FOOTPRINTS IN THE SNOW

A Pictorial Biography of
Josemaría Escrivá
The Founder of Opus Dei

By Dennis M. Helming

Foreword by Malcolm Muggeridge

Scepter Publishers
New York - London

Published in the United States by Scepter Publishers, Inc., 481 Main Street, New Rochelle, N. Y. 10801; in England by Scepter Ltd. 1 Leopold Road, London W5 3PB; in the Philippines by Sinag-tala Publishers, Inc. Greenhills, P.O. Box 536, Manila 3113.

Photo credits:
Front cover, 53, 54, and 68: Eric Streiff;
1 to 5, 7 to 12, 14 to 20, 22 to 31, 33, 34,
36 to 42, 44 to 53, and 67: *Bulletin on the Life of Msgr. Escriva.*

Typesetting and design by Graphics Plus, Port Chester, New York.

ISBN 0-933932-50-2

FOREWORD

By MALCOLM MUGGERIDGE

It is some years now since I first heard the words Opus Dei. Somehow the Latin spoke for itself: God's Work, this signifying, I supposed, all worthwhile work of every kind, ranging between a mother's tender care of her child, a ploughman preparing land for planting, a Michelangelo painting the Sistine Chapel, a labourer cleaning out sewers. True work is indeed holy. Witness George Herbert's beautiful lines of how working for God "makes drudgery divine":

> Teach me, my God and King
> In all things Thee to see,
> And what I do in anything
> To do it as for Thee.

The Apostle Paul, too, finds in his work to support himself a strengthening of his Evangel for Christ.

So much for the name, devised by Monsignor Escrivá, the only begetter of Opus Dei as we know it today, about whom the following pages have much to say: a holy man who yet holds onto the world rather than eschewing it; a priest who handles his youthful associates with great tact and spirit; like St. Francis, fond of laughter, and everyone's brother. I was shown some film of him in various postures, the last being the most striking: Monsignor Escrivá on a platform answering random questions from a large and variegated audience spread out before him. Superficially observed, it might have been a highly sophisticated talk show; more closely examined, underneath the badinage there was God's finger probing and loving. It all fitted in very well with Monsignor Escrivá's own definition of Opus Dei's special vocation: "contemplatives in the middle of the world."

In the eighteenth century the mystical Jesuit, Jean Pierre de Caussade, celebrated the Sacrament of the Present Moment. In the twentieth century, passing through and beyond that moment to cooperate with God in reworking creation, Monsignor Escrivá spoke of "The Richness of Ordinary Life," the marrow of Opus Dei. I cannot improve upon the words of Father John O'Connor, O.S.A.:

> 'The Richness of Ordinary Life' is the great man's message to this century, which he sought to bring back to Christ. At the heart of that richness is union with Christ, a union maintained by prayer and a purely spiritual dimension. But Monsignor Escrivá stressed again and again that the union

is also kept alive through the sanctification and especially through the conscious excellence of human work.

"I suppose," Father John goes on, "that [Monsignor Escrivá] spent his life trying to show the world how to harmonize the natural with the supernatural, God with Man and Man with God...and it is this example, as well as his teaching, that he leaves as a special legacy to his family in Opus Dei, to the Church and to the world."

Now I look back with great satisfaction on meeting Opus Dei people at home and abroad; for instance, at Wickenden Manor southwest of London, where I talked to some diocesan priests; then in New York and Washington, D.C. There were also visitors like Father Gonzalo Gonzalez, whom my wife Kitty and I came to hold in high esteem. The dedication of these young Christians to their vocation with Opus Dei and its begetter was in every respect edifying.

As it happens, the only Opus Dei V.I.P. I encountered was Gregorio López Bravo, when he was Foreign Secretary in the Spanish Government. I went to Madrid to meet him on behalf of the BBC, to record an interview with him. Our conversation got off to a good start when I asked him whether he began his day in the Foreign Office with a prayer. He said he did, in accordance with Opus Dei practice. I congratulated him on so doing; anything, I said, that induced a politician to put aside his Ego and turn to God was desirable. He agreed. Subsequently, I met his large family and went to Mass with them; altogether it was a pleasant occasion. Lately I was saddened to read his obituary in *The Times*, he having been killed in an air accident.

Here is a truly remarkable story, well told in this book. The growth and development of God's Work, which is also Man's; the realization in one mind that what appear to be the ordinary things of Time are images of the extraordinary things of Eternity. And behind it all one mind that will not be diverted from its purpose, one soul gathering to itself others similarly disposed—Monsignor Escrivá's.

Sussex, England
19 March, 1985

INTRODUCTION

I first stumbled upon Opus Dei in 1956 while an undergraduate. The place was improbable—and that is the key to understanding God's Work. It was at a college originally set up by New England Puritans, at the time feared to be a nest of Reds, and most certainly a haven for minds that had long since dismissed Christianity. It is better known as Harvard.

Yet there, studying or teaching in Cambridge, Massachusetts, was a handful of men—not even a dozen—who formed part of Opus Dei. They did not stand out because they were combative or cowed.

The striking thing about these ordinary, albeit talented, men, was, quite simply, their cheerfulness. They were optimistic and confident—persons who visibly regarded themselves as fortunate. It was almost as if they had been let in on a big secret: the Good News was compatible, not only with Harvard, but also with the personal shortcomings they shared with most mortals. Neither they nor their circumstances needed to be special, privileged or ethereal, for them to aspire to their full Christian inheritance. One only needed a trustworthy "coach" to make Christianity viable, practical, even it seemed fun. And in Opus Dei they had found that spiritual coach, nothing less.

There was about these young men an air of discovery and liberation. They, too, had once felt that to take God seriously would largely remove them from the world, while to take the world seriously would probably end up putting a damper on God. Opus Dei, they had come to see, could help them avoid an either-or choice. No wonder they were so eager—sometimes perhaps, understandably overeager—to see others, too, win in this supernatural sweepstakes.

And what was so special about this "coach" of theirs? Intuitively then, more explicitly later, I supposed it to be what has always characterized winning coaches: insistence on basics, little improvements, constancy, high goals, realistic practicality, patience, team spirit, straight talk, camaraderie, good habits, effort (more than winning)...But Opus Dei also seemed to have additional qualities not always found in athletic mentors: a premium on personal freedom and equal responsibility, lots of individualized attention, counsel and understanding, a family tone made up of real fraternity. Within this environment of cheerful self-forgetfulness and apostolic concern—"I'm not better, I've just been given more"—the gap separating ideals and reality could be faced and bridged little by little, without giving way to neurosis, despair and mere stoic doggedness. The game plan seemed to be: God will take care of the big things if you take care of the little ones; he'll take care of you if you take care of others.

Moreover, there was a sense of divine backing, an unspoken conviction that, despite *their* limitations and failings, Opus Dei was living up to its name and would continue to do so. They might not be up to achieving the desired outcome—in fact, they saw it as light years beyond their scant capabilities—but what did that matter? Weren't they but a brush in the hands of the Artist? And what fun to be conscious instruments in producing transcendent results!

Such were my initial impressions of this new spiritual phenomenon. These sporting apostles in Harris tweed jackets, so to speak, resembled the "new men" that C. S. Lewis had said would arise to perpetuate Christianity. I couldn't help but think—and the years since have reinforced that opinion—that Opus Dei was called upon to play a major role in righting an imbalance of long standing: the tradition that God could best be sought outside the world of work and family (as if God were not the very origin of that world quite as much as the sphere of otherworldly spirituality). If so—and the last five Popes seem to have shared that view—the man who gave birth to

Opus Dei deserves close scrutiny at least, and quite possibly gratitude.

A priest himself, Opus Dei's founder spent his life showing ordinary people that they need not necessarily embrace the clerical or religious state in order to embrace God. Josemaría Escrivá de Balaguer served up to lay folk all they needed to make the most, spiritually, of their condition in the world. His special calling as a priest was to help the laity discover their Christian vocation right where they had always been. (From the ranks of those same invigorated lay people, incidentally, would also come priests, brothers and nuns in abundance, refuting the notion that his emphasis would empty the seminaries and the convents.)

His was a *pastoral* change of emphasis, born of the conviction that God wants to befriend all persons so that they likewise will bring their friends within the reach of his friendship. Father Escrivá saw that the fundamental Christian calling was one, and therefore not only compatible with all honest circumstances, but meant to be the needed soul of every state in life, whether in the Church or in civil society.

When finally the world awakes from its binge of self-sufficiency, will it find that this race of "new men" loved it more than it could love itself, because they loved its Author still more, and thus learned how to bring the world to fruition? In that day, the name of Josemaría Escrivá would be a household word and more.

Then why so modest an account as this of the founder's life and works? Two reasons. First, to acquaint as broad a public as possible with this trailblazer. Second, it will take more time, resources and records than those available to me to compose anything approximating a definitive biography. I have opted for a sketch which, I hope, is faithful enough to its subject to whet appetites.

If the text is somewhat selective, I make no apologies for the accompanying photographs (which, unless otherwise noted, were generously made available by the editors of the *Bulletin on the Life of Monsignor Escrivá*).

I first met Opus Dei's founder in 1957. I last saw him during a trip to Rome in 1972. There were many other encounters during that 15-year span, all very real and vivid, none private. Those impressions have been supplemented by studying all his available writings and by viewing some 50 filmed documentaries of some of his pastoral work from 1972-75.

I was able to speak with many of the persons quoted. Also invaluable were the volumes, starting in 1954, of Opus Dei publications for members chronicling developments and, in recent years, offering historical recollections especially of the early years. I also relied on four tentative biographies: Salvador Bernal's *A Profile of Monsignor Escrivá*; Peter Berglar's *Opus Dei: Leben und Werk Seines Grunders*; François Gondrand's *Au Pas de Dieu*; and, above all, Andrés Vázquez de Prada's *El Fundador del Opus Dei*. Since mine, by contrast, is hardly a scholarly treatment, I have spared the reader the references for my numerous quotations.

No living organization with something serious to say about important matters escapes controversy. Opus Dei has surely not. However, a full discussion of these questions falls outside the limited scope of this book.

The story is that Monsignor Escrivá gave up on neither lay people nor God. In fact, the spiritual attention that Opus Dei gives to married people may well be his most far-reaching legacy. To strengthen the home may not change the world, but neither will it leave civil society and the Church the same.

NOT JUST A GOOD THING

Around 1935 Vicente Rodríguez, a young historian, cornered Father Escrivá, a priest only half a dozen years his senior. He was casting about for ways to make Christianity a more attractive proposition to his colleagues. Halfway through the academic's plans, Opus Dei's founder spoke up: "You have your ideas as to what we should do, and I have mine. If it were up to me, I would do things differently. But the important thing, the only thing, is that we do what God wants."

This wasn't the first time Father Escrivá had made it clear to a handful of followers that the Work was neither his nor Vicente's. Later in the decade he committed to print what he had often said before: "Bear in mind...you're not just a soul who has joined with other souls in order to do a good thing. That's a lot, but it's still little. You are the apostle who is carrying out an imperative command of Christ."

What kind of man was Father Escrivá that he should feel himself entrusted with doing God's Work? He saw himself as a "deaf and inept instrument...a poor sinner who loves Jesus Christ madly." And what was this Work laid on him? To spread this same "madness" among men and women in all walks of life.

Yes, that's right: in the middle of the world, "on Main Street," he liked to say. There lies the novelty, the revolution, if you will. What others saw as a stumbling block, he saw as a stepping stone. People didn't have to leave the world to find God. They could be men and women of the world, without being worldly. The key was to belong at the same time— and mainly—to God.

It's hardly surprising that a project to ransom the world from within would ruffle a few feathers. On the one hand, the modern world, with all its affluence, technical progress and education, has increasingly turned its back on religion. On the other, many religionists, hoping to stem the exodus from their temples, have been busily accommodating religion

[1] THE FOUNDER'S PARENTS DOLORES AND JOSE
Married in 1898, they made their home in Barbastro, Spain (1900 population: near 7,000), where Dolores, the second youngest of 13 children, had grown up. José died in 1924 at age 57; Dolores passed away at age 64 in 1941.

[2] THE ESCRIVA HOME ON MAIN STREET

This corner house (center) on Barbastro's Main Street witnessed the birth of five of the six Escrivá children, including Josemaría in 1902, and the childhood deaths of three daughters. Following financial ruin, the Escrivás moved in 1915 to Logroño, selling what had been their home for 17 years. An educational center entrusted to Opus Dei now occupies the building.

[3] EARLIEST PHOTO OF JOSEMARIA ESCRIVA

Dressed in the fashion typical of the early years of this century, Josemaría is shown at two years of age. In the same year, 1904, the boy fell gravely ill, and doctors saw no hope of his surviving. One night when it was not thought that he would reach morning, his mother promised the Virgin that the parents would take the boy, if cured, on a pilgrimage to the shrine of Our Lady of Torreciudad.

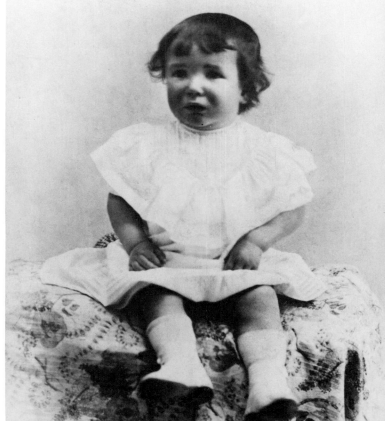

[4] THE FIRST PILGRIMAGE
Shown to the right of an abandoned signal tower is the ancient shrine, recently restored, dedicated to Our Lady of Torreciudad: an age-darkened wooden statue dating from at least the 11th century. The craggy, desolate site is found at the feet of the Pyrenees Mountains.

Early in the century, when Dolores Escrivá carried two-year-old Josemaría in her arms to the shrine in thanksgiving for his cure, it was accessible only on foot or horseback. The path was steep and bumpy, hemmed in by brambles and briers. A new shrine at the site, inaugurated with a funeral Mass for Opus Dei's founder in 1975, has since attracted millions of pilgrims.

to modern times and mores, thus heading in the opposite direction from Father Escrivá. (He sought to Christianize the world, not secularize Christianity.)

The result has been an increasingly flat world, consenting to God's exile, when not worse. Then an upstart priest challenges the world's self-sufficiency, not from some convent, monastery or rectory, but on the world's own turf: the field of work. To people who might feel trapped by "making a living," he offers the bonus of work-won heaven. Could this spiritually ambitious priest possibly make the obituaries of Christianity at least premature?

The story began in Spain, following an unnoticed event on October 2, 1928. The full name of the priest was Josemaría Escrivá de Balaguer (y Albás, if his mother's maiden name is affixed, as is the Spanish custom). The ideas he was spreading were the driving force behind Opus Dei (Latin for Work of God), a new institution in the Catholic Church, tailored for lay people. When he died on June 26, 1975, over 62,000 people of all kinds had committed themselves to living Christianity in the middle of the world by following his way. In 1981 the Vatican began studying whether this prodigious Spanish priest was a saint. What follows is a sketch of this man and what he did.

FIRST LOVE

[5] THE UNSUSPECTING TEENAGER
The portrait shows Josemaría when he was 15. Around his 16th birthday the high school senior sensed that God was calling him. Nearly 11 years, however, would have to pass before Josemaría's mission became clear. Meanwhile he resolved to become a diocesan priest, "because I thought it would be easier that way to fulfill whatever God wanted."

[6] SARAGOSSA 60 YEARS AGO

Saragossa is the capital of the northeast Spanish province of the same name, a role it inherited from the former kingdom of Aragon. It presides over a plain devoted to agriculture and bisected by the Ebro River. Shown is how it looked when Josemaría studied here for the priesthood (1920-25) and also served as a young priest (1925-27).

The church spires in the distance (center) belong to the cathedral of the Virgin of the Pillar. The name derives from a venerated pillar on which, according to popular devotion, the blessed Virgin appeared to the apostle St. James on his journey through Spain. Subsequently it has served as a pedestal for a statue of the Mother of God. During his Saragossa days Opus Dei's founder prayed before the image at least once a day.

Around Josemaría's 16th birthday (January 9, 1918), a heavy snowfall blanketed the small, north-central Spanish city of Logroño, where the Escrivás lived. Peering out the window early the next morning, the boy could see only an unsullied white carpet. As he hurried out to enjoy it, he saw something that merited a closer look. Somebody had been out before him. There leading off into the distance were footprints. Exactly that: not prints made by boots or shoes. The impressions were of bare feet, those of an unshod Carmelite from a nearby monastery [5] (numbers in brackets, like this one, identify related photographs and captions, which are presented in chronological order).

He later confided that the incident bore into him and set his mind and heart churning. If, he reasoned, that Carmelite can sacrifice himself out of love for God, what am I doing for the Lord? Wonder mingled with prayer awoke in the teenager a desire to do something for God.

As Josemaría tried to make out what that "something" was, he was visited now and then by what he called "intimations of Love"—special graces or lights. "There come to mind," he later said, "so many manifestations of God's love during my adolescent years, when I sensed that our Lord wanted something of me.... Ordinary events and happenings, seemingly without significance, yet he used them to plant within my soul a divine restlessness...they stirred and led me to daily communion, purification, confession and penance."

The cry of Bartimeus, the blind man in the Gospel —"Lord, that I may see"— became Josemaría's leitmotif. Hundreds of times a day he would ask for light.

It came, but gradually. By early springtime of that year he saw enough to conclude he was not called to follow the Carmelite, but rather should become a diocesan priest. "Because," he said, "I thought it would be easier that way to fulfill something God wanted, which I did not know. For about eight years before my ordination I had intimations of it, but I did not know what it was."

Till then Josemaría had only thought of becoming an architect. "When I was in secondary school," he confessed, "we studied Latin. I did not like it. In a silly way—how it pains me now—I used to say, 'Latin is for priests and monks....' You see how far away I was from wanting to be a priest.... I loved priests very much, because my upbringing at home was deeply religious; I had been taught to respect and venerate the priesthood. But it was not for me; it was for others."

Apparently the teen's father was also surprised. "One fine day," the son later recounted, "I told my father that I wanted to be a priest: it was the only time I saw him cry. He had other plans in mind, but he did not object. He told me, 'My son, think it over carefully. A priest has to be a saint.... It is very hard to have no house, no home, to have no love on earth. Think about it a bit more, but I will not oppose your decision'."

Later that spring Josemaría's father introduced him to two priests, friends of his, to help the 16-year-old with his spiritual life and ecclesiastical studies. During the two years following graduation from high school the young man attended the Logroño seminary, as a day student, supplementing that training at home with these two priests as his tutors.

[7] THE BROTHERS ESCRIVA IN 1921

Following his first year away from home at the Saragossa seminary, Josemaría spent part of the summer in Logroño. Sharing the park bench with him is Santiago. (At least during vacations it was then customary for Spanish seminarians to wear civilian dress.)

Santiago was born in 1919, the year following Josemaría's decision to become a priest and ten years after the birth of the Escrivá's last previous child, since deceased. At the time Dolores was 42 and her husband, 52, five years before his death. Josemaría's father had been counting on him to care for the family when he passed away. The older brother always saw Santiago's arrival as the answer to prayers: "With that event I touched God's grace with my hands; I saw it as a manifestation of our Lord."

[8] WITH FELLOW SEMINARIANS
Josemaría (seated, middle of front row) posed with his classmates at St. Francis de Paula Seminary in Saragossa in 1922. To differentiate themselves from other seminarians who attended the same pontifical university, those from St. Francis de Paula wore over their cassocks a red stole draped over their shoulders, adorned with a metallic "sun" embossed with the word *charitas*.

October, 1920: the handsome, sturdy youth of 18 transferred to St. Francis de Paula Seminary in Saragossa [6]. For the next four years he attended classes at the pontifical university [7, 8]. The seminary regimen was typical for the time. The seminarians meditated for half an hour before morning Mass. On the heels of breakfast they left for classes, in double file, accompanied by a superior. After an early-afternoon dinner back at St. Francis, they again reported to classes, followed by recreation, study and rosary. After supper they said prayers and listened to a brief talk. On Thursday afternoons they took walks, again in pairs.

In 1923, while still a seminarian, he began working for a civil law degree at the University of Saragossa, thus heeding a suggestion from his father. Was he thereby preparing himself better for whatever God might ask of him?

Josemaría was growing on the inside at least. He excelled at his theological studies. At least once a day he visited a favored shrine dedicated to Mary. Many a night he spent praying from a chapel balcony overlooking the tabernacle [9]. He kept his body in tow: fasting and sleeping on the floor, among other penances. Always he was trying to 'pester' God to reveal his plan.

A few months before his ordination he received word that his father was very ill, and he should hurry home. On alighting from the train back in Logroño, Josemaría learned the news: his father had died "from exhaustion."

The elder Escrivá had risen fit the morning of November 27, 1924. He ate breakfast and said his customary prayers before a small statue of the blessed Virgin. As he was about to leave the apartment and report to work, his heart gave out and he fell to the floor.

José Escrivá, 57, had worked hard and suffered much, especially during the last 15 years of his life. In 1915 he uprooted the family from their hometown of Barbastro [1-4] and moved to Logroño. Behind lay the graves of three daughters who had died from illness between 1910-13: first an infant, then a five-year-old, finally one who was eight. Also behind lay the debris of his ruined textile business, a victim of his partner's apparent chicanery. He had to let go the family servants and sell their comfortable home. Logroño represented a new start for José and Dolores, his wife of 17 years, but with greatly reduced means. The best he could offer her and their two remaining children was a cramped apartment, short on conveniences, hot in summer, chilly in winter. Try as he might at the same line of business in Logroño, José Escrivá barely improved the finances of his family. But the example of his cheerful sacrifice was not lost on the other Escrivás.

Josemaría was close to his parents; his father was his "best friend." They allowed him considerable freedom from an early age, while discreetly keeping a close watch on him and leaving his pockets relatively empty. "I can never recall having seen [my father] look severe," he said. "I remember him always calm, with a smiling face. And he died worn out...but he was always smiling. I owe my vocation to him."

Dolores taught her children the faith and prayers. "Every morning and night I recite the prayers my mother taught me," the son claimed some six decades later. "She was always busy with something: knitting or sewing or mending clothes or reading....There was nothing odd about her; she was normal, kind...a good mother who cared for her family, a Christian family, and she knew how to make good use of her time."

Recollections of his mother may have colored one of his homilies: "How many mothers have you known who have been the heroines of some epic or extraordinary event? Few, very few. Yet you and I know many mothers who are indeed heroic, truly heroic, who have never figured in anything spectacular, who will never hit the headlines, as they say. They lead lives of constant self-denial, happy to curtail their own lives and preferences, their time...so that they can carpet their children's lives with happiness."

On March 28, 1925, Josemaría received holy orders as a priest. Then began a struggle that was to last for years: he loved the Mass so much that he had to struggle against his tendency to prolong it. Following his first assignment in a small village [10], Father Josemaría lived in Saragossa, with his mother, sister Carmen and brother Santiago. (In Spain where rectories are scarce, most priests live with members of their family.) But they didn't see as much of him as they might have hoped. He continued his civil law studies. He tutored, which brought in some money to help support the family. He persuaded law school classmates to help teach catechism in some of Saragossa's slums. And then, of course, he administered the sacraments and preached in area churches, among other priestly assignments.

Some eight years had now gone by since the jolt occasioned by those snowy footprints. Meanwhile Father Josemaría's prayers had won from God what he called "operative graces." Whatever else they were, some at least were inspirations: glimpses of light, apostolic panoramas, hints of more to come. As best he could, the young priest would jot them down and date each piece of paper.

With the permission of Saragossa's archbishop, in May, 1927, Father Escrivá moved with his family to Madrid—the only city in Spain where he could then obtain a doctorate in civil law. In the capital he also expected to find a larger, more promising setting for the apostolic venture that God had yet to disclose.

Circumstances, however, were anything but favorable. Madrid was a teeming city of nearly one million, most of them recent arrivals from the farm whose shantytowns encircled the city. There was plenty of political ferment. The cauldron progressively heated up in the thirties, boiling over in 1936 with the outbreak of the civil war.

Amid the turmoil Father Josemaría continued his tasks—at a faster tempo, if anything. He prayed, tutored in law, worked at his doctoral tasks at the University of Madrid, served as chaplain in a church. Above all he devoted himself to the poor, the ignorant and the critically ill with works of mercy, tendered always with a smile, sometimes with disarming humor. Thousands of confessions: many for the first time, almost as many for the last; preparing urchin and orphan alike for first communion, again in the thousands; comforting the sick or dying, whether in bulging ward or abandoned hovel; crisscrossing Madrid on foot, rosary in hand, cardboard in spent shoe.

From this time comes a telling story. Father Escrivá taught Roman and canon law at an academy. One day

[9] A CENTERPIECE FOR JOSEMARIA
From 1920 to 1925 this baroque church and especially its tabernacle were the focus for many of Josemaría's waking hours. Here with the other seminarians he meditated, attended Mass and benediction and prayed the rosary. On many a night besides, Josemaría would keep a prayerful vigil from a balcony on the right side overlooking the sanctuary.

In this church he was ordained a priest on March 28, 1925 and gave holy communion to his mother for the first time. Following the death of Josemaría's father the preceding November, Mrs. Escrivá, along with Carmen and five-year-old Santiago, had moved to Saragossa.

[10] FIRST A RURAL PRIEST

A recent photo shows the house (indicated by a cross above the door) where the new priest lived during his first assignment, beginning the day following his First Mass. Perdiguera is a small farming village some 15 miles from Saragossa. For six weeks Father Josemaría substituted for the pastor, who had taken sick. He lodged in the home of "a very good man," in his words.

a fellow teacher revealed to the students something of the priest's extracurricular activities. The students didn't believe it. What was such an urbane, eloquent and even elegant professor, admittedly a priest, doing with the proletariat? The claim must be a joke or at best an exaggeration. A bet ensued. After class they stealthily followed the priest-professor. The incredulous students lost more than shoe leather, as they tailed Father Escrivá on his rounds through the slums of Madrid.

Doubtless the young priest reasoned that by thus living his priesthood, he was preparing himself to respond to God's definitive call. Perhaps in this way he might even hurry it along.

DIVINE ERUPTION

As he did every year, Father Escrivá was spending some days of spiritual retreat at a residence run by religious near the heart of Madrid. On the morning of October 2, 1928, he closeted himself in his room to mull over the papers on which he had recorded the partial messages he had received from God during the past decade. At a given moment he "saw," as he put it, in all its extension and depth what was later to be named Opus Dei [11, 12].

From that moment on, the 26-year-old priest understood that persons of all conditions and backgrounds could and should effectively aspire to a full Christian life in and through their ordinary activities. He also understood that he was to be instrumental in calling

[11] THE BIRTH OF OPUS DEI
October 2, 1928, feast of the Holy Guardian Angels: the 26-year-old priest was making a retreat at a residence of the Missionaries of St. Vincent de Paul (Vincentians) in Madrid, shown as it looked then. While reviewing in his room papers on which over the years he had recorded inspirations, Father Escrivá "saw" Opus Dei as God wanted it to be, projected through the centuries.

the laity to give themselves to God by following a clearly defined path to holiness and apostolate that wove its way through their secular occupations and preoccupations.

Always reticent to go into greater detail, the vision was partially outlined in an interview he gave to the *New York Times* in 1966:

Our Lord gave rise to Opus Dei in 1928 to remind Christians that, as we read in the book of Genesis, God created man to work. We have come to call attention once again to the example of Jesus, who spent 30 years in Nazareth, working as a carpenter. In his hands, a professional occupation, similar to that carried out by millions in the world, was turned into a divine task. It became a part of our redemption, a way to salvation.

The spirit of Opus Dei reflects the marvelous reality (forgotten for centuries by many Christians) that any honest and worthwhile work can be converted into a divine occupation. In God's service there are no second class jobs; all of them are important.

To love and serve God, there is no need to do anything strange or extraordinary. Christ bids all without exception to be perfect as his heavenly Father is perfect (cf. Mt 5:48). Sanctity, for the vast majority of people, implies sanctifying their work, sanctifying themselves in it, and sanctifying others through it. Thus they can encounter God in the course of their daily lives. The conditions of contemporary society, which places an ever higher value on work, evidently make it easier for the people of our times to understand this aspect of the Christian message, which the spirit of the Work has recalled.

The earliest members of the Work all tell of their initial amazement at the scope and detail with which the founder spoke to them of this new way, when there was quite literally nothing to point to. It was obvious to them that Opus Dei had not been born in response to particular difficulties then menacing their country or Church. The vistas that the young priest painted for them were not bounded by time or space.

And Father Josemaría would cheerfuly reassure them that they had means aplenty to pursue it: "the Gospel and the Cross."

For centuries it had been generally felt that a life centered on God required certain safeguards and incentives to ensure sufficient disentanglement from the world: withdrawal into the cloister; vows of chastity, poverty and obedience; distinctive garb; a rule prescribing practices of prayer, penance and silence; immersion in the liturgy, sacraments and so on.

Thus, almost imperceptibly, the essence of Christian life came in practice to be identified with prescriptions laid down for religious by founders of the monastic orders: an otherworldly setting for sacred pursuits. Pious diocesan priests tried to model their lives, as best they could, on the monastic pattern, though frequently they lowered their sights owing to their greater exposure to the world.

Given the laity's still skimpier fare and still greater distractions and temptations, churchmen tended to expect less of ordinary Christians. And lay people responded accordingly, often pessimistic about attempting much more than fitful observance of the ten commandments and the Church's laws. Those lay people (usually women) who went beyond these precepts in their sundry devotions and sacramental usages were the pride and joy of their priestly mentors.

Such was the clerically top-heavy tradition of the Church universal, accentuated if anything in Spain before and after the civil war. But do lay people have to settle for second or third best? In urging them to go higher, Father Escrivá was more optimistic about both the power of God's grace and the generosity of the "man in the street."

Ricardo F. Vallespín, then an architecture student, recalls his first encounter with Father Josemaría: "He spoke in a way totally new to me about things of the soul, about spiritual matters. His words set my heart afire and provoked a deep determination to improve."

[12]...MEANWHILE, A PEALING OF BELLS

Asked in 1974 why he began Opus Dei, the founder replied: "Opus Dei is not mine. I've often had to ask pardon of my children for not having been a good instrument. I did not want to found it because I was a coward. But now I'm full of joy, and from that October 2nd of 1928 there still sounds in my ears the pealing of some bells, those of the church of Our Lady of the Angels in Madrid," being rung that very day.

In October, 1972, the only remaining bell was offered to the founder. He told its story: "The Communists heaved the bells of the church of Our Lady of the Angels to the street from the bell tower. All the bells broke except for one. That bell was presented to me by the clergy of Madrid—the pastor, the cardinal and his bishops—and it is now in Torreciudad. When holy Mass is celebrated on the esplanade, the bell of Our Lady of the Angels will ring at the moment of consecration."

The bell is shown in its new home, close to an outdoor altar.

"The easiest way to understand Opus Dei," the founder told *Time* years later, "is to consider the life of the early Christians. They lived their Christian vocation seriously, seeking earnestly the holiness to which they had been called by their baptism. Externally they did nothing to distinguish themselves from their fellow citizens. The members of Opus Dei are ordinary people. They work like everyone else and live in the midst of the world just as they did before they joined. There is nothing false or artificial about their behavior. They live like any other Christian citizen who wants to respond fully to the demands of his faith."

Wouldn't the Christian message have to be watered down to attract Tom, Dick and Harry? No, replied Father Escrivá. This was the secret: "The more you are in the world, the more you must be in God." He had seen this clearly, ever since that autumn morning in 1928. It took others a little longer—and quite understandably—to appreciate Opus Dei's message.

Listen to the account of Victor G. Hoz, a young married man and psychologist who later joined Opus Dei: "Father Josemaría told me one day in 1941, 'God is calling you to paths of contemplation.' I was amazed. I had always thought that to be a contemplative was for holy people given to the mystical way of life, to be aimed at only by a chosen few, by people for the most part withdrawn from the world. But I was a married man, with three children, and expecting to have more (which was in fact what happened), and I had to work hard to support my family."

Throughout his life Opus Dei's founder always sought out those who were "too busy," who had no time left over for the supposed luxury of cultivating a spiritual life. Their industriousness and self-discipline conditioned them to discover nobler aims that could better sustain—not replace—their pursuits. On the other hand, those who shied away from the requirements of human excellence would have to mend their easy-going ways before they could enter into Opus Dei's promise and program.

In many ways Opus Dei represents a throwback to the original plan: God's first command, laid on Adam and Eve, was "Be fruitful and multiply; fill the earth and *subdue* it" (Gen 1:28). Father Escrivá reminded any who would listen that things human are not merely mundane: they come from God. And man ratifies God's will by obediently working well for God's sake. Thus does Opus Dei's founder describe the central setting of work in this lay vocation: "to sanctify one's work, to sanctify oneself in that work, to sanctify others by means of that work." When that happens, work assumes for Father Escrivá the traits of a benign disease: "progressive, incurable and contagious."

Does this revaluation of human activity go overboard? The danger of creating a monstrous hybrid (attempting to yoke religiosity and secularity) would be real if all this activity were not grounded in contemplation. "Prayer is the secret of Opus Dei—not work," insisted Father Escrivá. "Thus we must convert our work into prayer." If not, perseverance would be out of the question, he would add. For him work is an invitation to convert all human pursuits into a prayerful dialogue of virtuous deeds and conversation with one's Father God. Doing so, doubtless, also involves no little share of self-denial and penance. Thus the essence of full Christian life—union with Christ in the sacraments, prayer, mortification and apostolate—has been put within reach of the vast majority of mankind, who need not feel slighted or guilty amid secular pursuits. If the far-reaching aims and program of Opus Dei were to catch on, might not the long-standing "mistrust" between the world and God end up a thing of the past?

How does one maintain allegiance to God in the thick of everyday life? What Father Josemaría wrote in *The Way* offers some clues. First he gets readers used to the idea; then he coaxes them to make it more than an idea. A sampling:

- I'll tell you a secret, an open secret: these world crises are crises of saints. God wants a handful of men "of his own" in every human activity. Then... "the peace of Christ in the kingdom of Christ."
- You have the obligation to sanctify yourself. Yes, even you! Who thinks this is the exclusive concern of priests and religious? To everyone, without exception, our Lord said: "Be perfect, as my heavenly Father is perfect."
- Work! When you are engrossed in professional work, the life of your soul will improve, and you'll become more of a man for you'll get rid of that "carping spirit" that consumes you.
- What amazes you seems quite natural to me. God has sought you out right in the midst of your work. That is how he sought the first, Peter and Andrew, John and James, beside their nets, and Matthew, sitting in the custom-house....

- "Was not our heart burning within us, while he spoke to us on the way?" If you are an apostle, these words of the disciples of Emmaus should rise spontaneously to the lips of your professional companions when they meet you along the way of their lives.

In many ways Opus Dei does represent a novelty within the Church's life. Although the essential, God-centered Christian vocation remains the same, the setting for working it out as proposed by Opus Dei—the world—is relatively untested as a context for the sustained pursuit of sanctity. In this regard its founder says, "Opus Dei is as old as the Gospel and, like the Gospel, new." But he would also point out that there are ample precedents for Opus Dei's spirit and style of life among the Christians of the earliest centuries, who likewise did not abandon the world. Despite these antecedents, however, the Work of God, when seen against the 15 centuries when the monastic ideal reigned, is a bold, new enterprise. Is it any wonder, then, that it was to meet with skepticism and misunderstanding?

FIRST STEPS

After that October 2, Opus Dei's founder later confided, "I never had any *tranquillity*, and I began to work — reluctantly, because I did not like the idea of being the founder of anything...I began to work, to move, to do: to lay the foundations." God had opened his eyes to unsuspected horizons, but he had provided no road map, no co-workers, no material means. Father Josemaría made inquiries about some recent Catholic organizations in Central Europe and Italy. If one of them matched what God had shown him, he was ready to join and take the last place. As information reached him, however, it became clear that he was to break ground alone.

To say it wasn't easy is understatement indeed. Decades later Father Escrivá confessed that if God had shown him all at once what he would have to suffer to give birth to this new spiritual family, "I would have died." But "God led me by the hand, quietly, little by little, until his *castle* was built: take that step, he seemed to say, put that there, take that away from here in front and put it over there. That is the way our Lord has built his Work."

What was going through the young founder's mind? "I had my twenty-six years," he said, "God's grace, a good sense of humor, and nothing else. But just as men write with a pen, our Lord writes with a table leg to make it clear that it is he who is doing the writing. That is what is so incredible, so marvelous. All the theological and ascetical doctrine had to be created. I found before me a break in continuity, a gap of centuries: there was nothing. Humanly speaking, the whole Work was a crazy venture. That is why some people said that I was mad, and that I was a heretic, and so many other things besides."

At the beginning Father Josemaría's routine and duties remained apparently the same [13]. But a close observer would have noticed a greater resolve, manifested in his constant search for persons who would pray "for a special intention of mine." Seeing himself

[13] MADRID: OPUS DEI'S CRADLE
Shown is Alcalá Street, one of Madrid's main thoroughfares, as it appeared in 1931, three years after Opus Dei's founding and five years before the civil war. To attend to the sick and needy throughout the city and in outlying slums, Father Josemaría, usually too short on pesetas to use the trolley, was a frequent pedestrian here.

[14] THE CHAPLAIN'S MARCHING ORDERS

Soon after Father Escrivá reached the Spanish capital in 1927, he began to serve as chaplain to the Foundation for the Sick, established earlier in the decade by a new religious congregation known as the Apostolic Women of the Sacred Heart. Shown is but a small sample of the hundreds of preserved notes from the sisters telling him of people in need of his spiritual ministry. One can see on some of them the numbers he jotted down in organizing his route through various neighborhoods of Madrid.

One of the notes reads: "Please be good enough to visit a sick man at no. XX Fernández Street, who doesn't want to go to confession, but has agreed to your visiting him. It's quite urgent, for he was unconscious for several days and it's feared he'll become so again...."

One of the sisters later recalled, "I can't remember a single case where sick persons attended by Father Escrivá died without the sacraments."

as "a beggar of prayers," he turned above all to the sick and dying who agreed to offer up their sufferings and death for this unspecified purpose.

In the late twenties and early thirties, besides his tasks as Opus Dei's founder, Father Escrivá served as chaplain to a charitable undertaking known as the Foundation for the Sick [14]. It had been started several years before by a group of dedicated Catholic women. One of them, Sister Asunción Muñoz, recently testified:

"It was a blessing for us to have Father Escrivá as chaplain. I remember well our apostolic activities in the impoverished areas of Madrid. The hospitals were overcrowded, and many of the sick died at home. We sought out the gravest and neediest cases to help both spiritually and materially.

"In that environment Father Escrivá was indispensable. He thought nothing of sacrificing his time and himself to attend to the huge number of sick and poor. Whenever we came across someone about to die bereft of God's grace, we always called on Father Escrivá. I can't remember a single case where sick persons attended by Father Escrivá died without the sacraments.

"He dedicated himself to each soul with no sign of haste, as if he had nothing else to do. He visited them, bringing them communion and the other sacraments. Moreover, he would visit our schools, located in the slums, 58 of them with some 12,000 children. He would give talks and speak winningly with the children, engaging all his personal charm and energy as an apostle to bring them to the knowledge and love of Jesus Christ."

Then there were visits to public hospitals, certainly no models of hygiene with their overcrowded wards and corridors. All too often spirits matched the bodies. Religious ignorance and anticlericalism led patients to view any priest with hostility. Dr. Tomás Canales, an attending physician, says, "From the day I was first introduced to Father Escrivá, I used to see him frequently at the hospital in the morning throughout 1933-34. He went from ward to ward, speaking with the patients, hearing their confessions and giving them communion. He was not afraid of catching their diseases, most of them contagious. More than once he was warned of the risks, but he always answered, with his habitual smile, that he was immune to everything."

One day early in the thirties while ministering to the sick, Father Josemaría learned that a man was dying of tuberculosis in difficult circumstances. The victim was the brother of a prostitute and was bedridden in the bordello. How could he avoid scandal and still tend to the man's soul? He consulted the diocese's vicar general, who gave his permission. He pressed into service as his acolyte the brother-in-law of a countess: a man whose bearing and distinction

[15] WHERE TO GATHER?

The sign over this door translates as "The Little Basement."
The other two signs advertise ice cream and hot chocolate.
Here, in the absence of a place to call his own, the founder
gathered often with small groups of his followers. While
treating them to a snack, he fanned their apostolic desires.
He became so well known in the establishment that Angel,
the owner's son, on seeing them, would say, "Here he is,
with his disciples."

Because money then—as always—was scarce, the priest
would find an excuse not to snack himself. But the out-
lay often meant that he had to skip other meals besides.
Apparently no one realized, not even his family.

To chat with just one of the young men, Father Josemaría
would use the sidewalks and park benches.

reinforced his advanced years. He got the dying man's
sister to promise that on the morrow God would not
be offended in that house. The following day he heard
the man's confession, administered the last rites and
viaticum, and saw the man prayerfully through his
agony.

"The only time I desired to die," he admitted in
1974, referring to another instance, "was for a few
moments at the bedside of a dying young man, being
myself a young priest. I was envious of him. I said,
'You're going straight to heaven.' I thought those
words would console him, as they did."

Not unlike Diogenes, Opus Dei's founder was also
looking at this time for persons who would commit
themselves to the divine task he'd been given [15].
Where would these vocations be found? Among "the
sick, God's favorites, and those with big hearts, even
though their weaknesses had been bigger," he wrote in
1934. While devoting most of his time to those needy
in soul or body, whenever possible he would bring
along to the hospitals or catechism classes a small
group of college students, workers or young professionals [16].

25

[16] TEACHING OTHERS TO SERVE

A photo of the period shows a hospital that Father Josemaría and his followers would visit. Known as Madrid's General Hospital, it was next door to St. Elizabeth's Foundation and Convent, where in 1931 he became chaplain and later rector. The new position allowed him to devote more time to Opus Dei's development. His concern to serve the needy of soul and body found a new outlet next door to the church. He shared that concern with his young followers, who also volunteered for this service.

His attentions were not unappreciated. When he was announced in the hospital, a sister then working there recalls, word would spread through the wards, "Father Josemaría's back." Faces would light up.

Experience had taught Father Josemaría that serving the destitute and sick would benefit not only them, but also his youthful followers. He organized volunteer work in the hospitals. He and the young men talked with the sick and tried to cheer them up; they made their beds, washed their feet, cut their nails and combed their hair; they cleaned bed pans.... Afterwards Father Josemaría would accompany the young men to a nearby park. He would fan their idealism, lead them to seek greater intimacy with God and, as a consequence, to be useful to others. After years of this work, the founder could later claim that "Opus Dei was born among the poor and sick of Madrid's hospitals."

The founder recounted a related incident: "I remember someone from a well-known family. I can speak about him now because he has been in heaven for many years. He was one of the first members in those earliest years of Opus Dei. He took a chamber pot from the bedside of a tuberculosis patient. It was...well... But I told him, 'Go ahead and clean it.' But then, because the look of revulsion on his face made me regret what I had said, I followed him out of the room. And I found him cleaning the pot with his bare hand, his face beaming wonderfully."

The story of Luis Gordon later appeared in *The Way*: "Isn't it true, Lord, that you were greatly consoled by the childlike remark of that man, who, disconcerted by having to obey in something unpleasant and repulsive, whispered to you, 'Jesus, may I put on a good face'?"

Something happened to Father Josemaría on February 14, 1930, that led to his shouldering another huge commitment. When the young priest "saw" Opus Dei over a year before, he had not discerned the presence of women. He therefore concluded that he was to limit himself to working with men, and so he did. But God had other plans. Some 16 months after the start of Opus Dei, he saw during Mass, after communion, that Opus Dei was to have a second branch —for women. "As soon as Mass was over," Father Josemaría later confided, "I went running to see my confessor, who said to me, 'This is as much from God as the other'." Again, God left the "how" in the hands of the momentarily quaking priest.

In 1931 Father Josemaría volunteered to serve as chaplain to a community of contemplative nuns at the convent church of St. Elizabeth, where in 1934 he became rector. His new duties gave him more time to dedicate to Opus Dei's growth. (Not surprisingly, next door to the church was a bonus: a large, overcrowded hospital.) St. Elizabeth's central location facilitated

[17] OPUS DEI'S FIRST HOME

The photo shows a bronze plaque that identified Opus Dei's first home, a small rented apartment in Madrid that opened its doors in December, 1933. The Academy DYA catered to university students, especially those of law and architecture (whence the initials: *Derecho y Arquitectura*; in the founder's mind they also stood for God and Daring: *Dios y Audacia*). There were review classes and tutorials, in addition to a quiet study room. Here students could also participate in the classes in Christian living, launched in January, 1933, and chat personally with Father Josemaría about spiritual and apostolic matters.

Renting the apartment, while a helpful and productive move, was also a bold one, because expenses were considerable and income scant.

The plaque was later transferred twice. In the fall of 1934 it was moved to a new site with not only academic facilities but also living accommodations for a small number of college students, most of whom were not members of the Work. It identified the first academy-residence for two years. In the summer of 1936 it was moved to a larger academy-residence, but the outbreak of the Spanish civil war in mid-July put an end to plans to open the new center for the school year 1936-37.

[18] OPUS DEI'S FIRST TABERNACLE
Six years went by before Father Josemaría's dream for Opus Dei to have its own tabernacle and chapel were fulfilled in the new academy-residence, opened in the fall of 1934. To overcome obstacles he turned to St. Joseph: "In the depths of my soul I was already devoted to St. Joseph, a devotion I have inculcated in you. I recalled that other Joseph, to whom, following the Pharaoh's advice, the Egyptians turned in their hunger for good bread. *Ite ad Ioseph*: 'Go to Joseph' so that he might give you wheat. I began to ask St. Joseph to grant us the first tabernacle."

the first steps of his work with women. In one of its confessionals he introduced a growing number of young women to the spiritual life, leading them up an inclined plane of Christian dedication. Women who saw others lined up outside his confessional would join the queue....

Working with women, however, presented a somewhat different challenge. While they were called to the same spiritual program, forming them in it involved certain difficulties. In those days women enjoyed little freedom of movement. Neither was it customary then for young women to attend a university or enter the professions.

Even though many of the early followers of Father Escrivá abandoned him, as he put it, "without even saying good-bye," he did not lose heart. Some began to understand and commit themselves. One of the first was Isidoro Zorzano, an engineer who worked for a Spanish railroad in the Mediterranean port city of Málaga. Isidoro and Josemaría had been high school classmates in Logroño and had exchanged an occasional letter since their ways parted some ten

years before. One early summer day in 1930 Isidoro received a note from his former companion, the priest-lawyer: "When you come to Madrid, don't fail to look me up. I have some interesting things to tell you...."

In the preceding months Isidoro had been more pensive than usual. He suspected that God was inviting him to draw closer, yet he already had a vocation as an engineer, a calling he liked and discharged well. He felt no attraction to either the priesthood or the religious life. Was this because he was too worldly and cowardly to heed God's call? Or were these conflicting tugs just a passing fancy? Maybe Father Josemaría could shed some light on his predicament. Near the end of that summer, professional matters would take Isidoro to Madrid, where he could air his innermost thoughts with his friend.

The meeting almost didn't come off. Unable to forewarn Father Escrivá of his exact schedule, Isidoro went early to the priest's lodgings only to find him out and his whereabouts and timetable unknown. Maybe this was a sign that he was chasing the wind.

Since his business appointment was not until later in the day, Isidoro began to wander on foot through the streets, which, like his life, seemed to lead nowhere. Looking up from the sidewalk at one point, however, he thought he recognized the gait of a cassock-clad figure in front of him. Could it be? He broke into a trot and pulled abreast with a delighted "Josemaría!" There ensued a long, heartfelt conversation.

From August 24, 1930 on, Isidoro was to be God's engineer. He remained in Málaga until 1936, when he moved to Madrid. During Spain's civil war and in the years immediately following, he dedicated himself to Opus Dei's development. When he died in 1943 at 41 of Hodgkin's disease [39], he had lived the spirit of the Work so well that it was not long before his process of beatification was opened.

Death was no stranger to Opus Dei's thin ranks in the early days. Tuberculosis, then incurable, claimed in 1933 the life of the first woman member, María Escobar. About the same time Luis Gordon [16], another member, also an engineer, unexpectedly died. In circumstances that suggest poisoning by an anti-clerical fanatic, so too did Father José María Somoano, who worked closely with the founder.

Yet they had learned from Father Josemaría not only how to live, but also how to die well: cheerfully offering their lives for the good of the Church and the growth of Opus Dei. They got their way. Increasing numbers of young men and women were taking the first step: seeking spiritual guidance and instruction from Father Josemaría.

In January 1933, Opus Dei's founder started giving a series of weekly classes in practical Christian living to college students. Only three came to the first class, but within a week or two they were teaching catechism on Sunday mornings to poor children. Participants in Father Josemaría's classes were also encouraged to bring others. When a group reached ten or so, he would divide it and the *two* groups would start growing all over again. Within three years he was giving several classes every day.

"Only three came," the founder later said, recalling the beginnings of this venture. "'What a calamity!' you would have thought. Well, no! I was very optimistic, very happy, and I went to the sisters' chapel [the class took place in a room of an orphanage where Father Escrivá helped out.] I placed our Lord in the monstrance and gave benediction to those three. I seemed to see that the Lord Jesus, our God, was blessing three hundred, three hundred thousand, thirty million…white, black, yellow…of all the colors and combinations that human love can produce."

Throughout 1933 Father Escrivá continued to work on a small book of points for meditation to help his followers go deep in their prayer life. *Spiritual Consider-*ations came out in 1934. In 1939 it was amplified and reissued as *The Way*. Some 40 years later over three million copies in 35 languages were in circulation.

With money from God knows where, in the last month of 1933 Father Escrivá rented a small apartment as a first home for his apostolic activities. It was known as Academy DYA, letters that stood for law and architecture [17]. Students would go there to study or be tutored. Many also stayed to talk with the young priest. Everyone was also invited to pitch in to help make the cramped apartment more attractive and homelike.

"Up to this point," says the architect Ricardo F. Vallespín, "we used to see Father Escrivá in the apartment he shared with his mother, sister and brother. I had been in the Work only a little over a month at this time, but I'll never forget the first steps in my vocation, when our founder was introducing us to the ways of interior life. He spoke to us about the need to be saints in the middle of the world and to place Christ at the peak of all human activities. He transmitted to us his gigantic faith that all this panorama would become a reality. We didn't doubt for a moment that his words would come true, because that was God's will.

"Father Escrivá was keenly interested in the new apartment, because he saw it as a useful vehicle to form us and to expand the apostolic work with young men. He wasn't fazed by the shortage of material means, although upon his shoulders fell the burden of finding them. The apartment brought in little money and entailed plenty of expenses."

Father Josemaría acquired some furniture that belonged to his mother and other pieces from a family friend. "Each day," the founder later confessed, "when I was leaving my mother's house, my brother Santiago would come up and put his hands in my pockets and ask, 'What are you taking today to your nest?'"

"The apartment was relatively small," relates Ri-

[19] EARLY FOLLOWERS AND FRIENDS

The photo corresponds to school year 1935-36 at the academy-residence DYA. The founder is surrounded by both residents and other students who frequented the center. Alvaro del Portillo, his eventual successor who joined Opus Dei in July, 1935, stands at the end of the third row on the right.

cardo, now a priest. "It had a visitors' room, two small classrooms, a study room, a small living room and an office for our founder. And I can't forget the famous kitchen where Father Josemaría heard so many confessions—the other rooms were always occupied. With the new apartment we saw our founder much more, since he spent considerable time there, despite his many other occupations. The rest of us spent as much time there as we could manage.

"In his simple office at the Academy there was a bare, wooden cross, which invited him to pray and which he often alluded to when imparting spiritual guidance to so many students. He would teach us that we were to be bound out of love to that cross in the same way that Jesus had been nailed to it. He insisted that we must embrace Christ's cross in the midst of our ordinary duties and everyday occupations.

"At times he would arrive as tired as could be; it pained me to see him so exhausted. But somehow drawing strength from weakness, he would pull himself together and begin to see fellows. And always with his attractive smile and overflowing with good humor, he made life so pleasant for those at his side."

José Luis Múzquiz, then an engineering student, described his first conversation with Father Josemaría, after which he began to attend those practical sessions in Christian living. Right after the civil war he joined Opus Dei and later was ordained—eventually becoming known to many people in the United States as Father Joseph, for many years the counselor of Opus Dei in the U.S.

"We talked for about an hour," Múzquiz recalled. "The things our founder said struck deep; for example, 'The only love is God's love; other loves are tiny.' He spoke to me about the naturalness we should live. He commented that it wasn't a question of secrecy, but that it would be stupid to go around with a sign on our backs saying we were trying to be good. He then told me that there were these classes to which people came to listen, not to argue. One prepared the topic, and the others tried not only to listen, but to apply it to their lives.

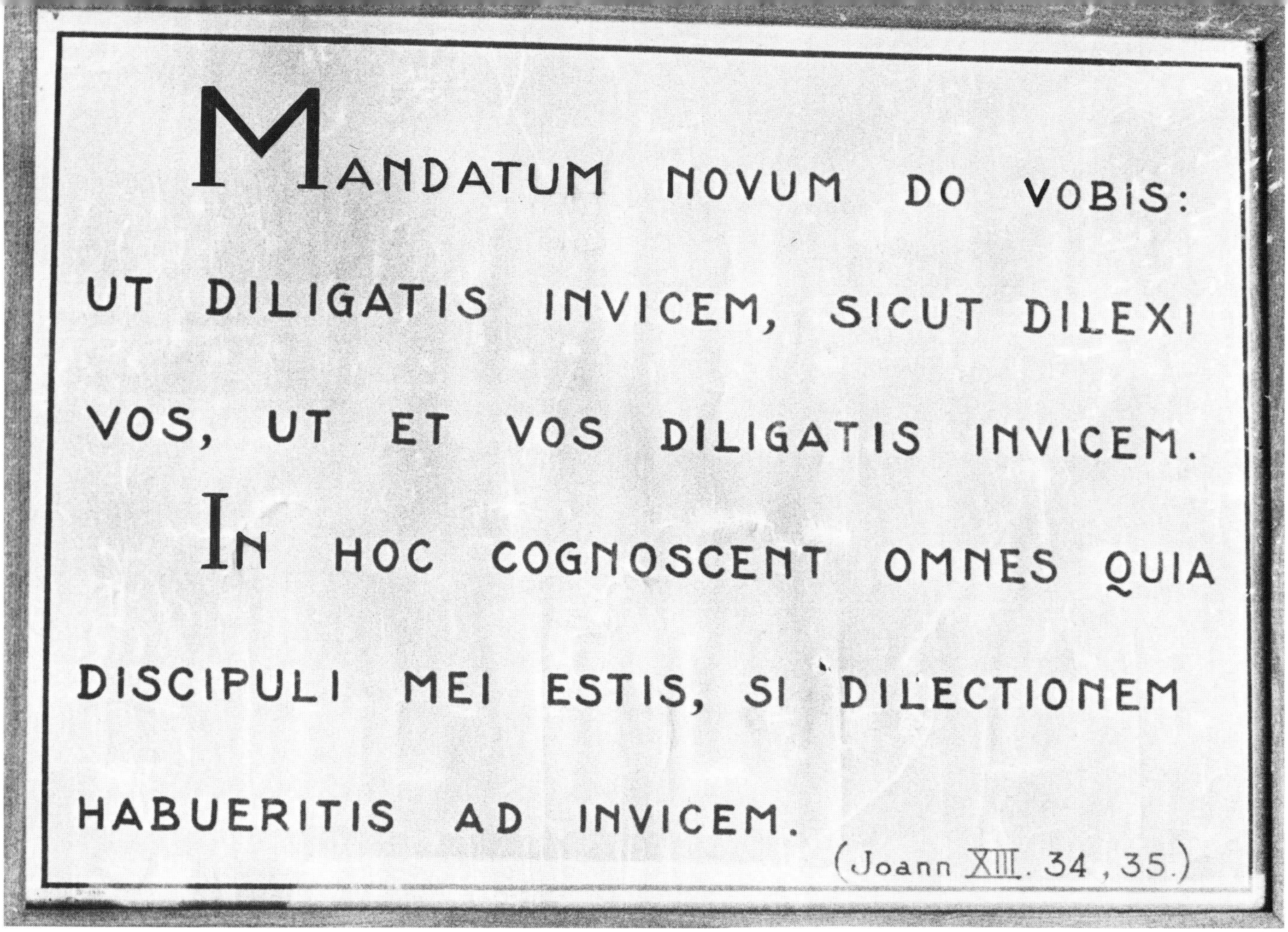

MANDATUM NOVUM DO VOBIS: UT DILIGATIS INVICEM, SICUT DILEXI VOS, UT ET VOS DILIGATIS INVICEM. IN HOC COGNOSCENT OMNES QUIA DISCIPULI MEI ESTIS, SI DILECTIONEM HABUERITIS AD INVICEM.

(Joann XIII. 34, 35.)

[20] RECURRING THEME

In conversation and preaching alike, one of Father Josemaría's most frequent topics was charity: fraternity, understanding, service, friendship, "deeds". ...He would claim that Christ's New Commandment, tendered at the Last Supper, was still new for so many who had yet to put it into practice.

To keep the goal before others' eyes, he had the text of the commandment framed and placed in the study room of Opus Dei's modest first center: "...In this will all men know that you are my disciples, if you have love for one another." Thus was born a tradition.

Shown here is the second hand-lettered Latin text prepared for the academy-residence that was never opened because of the outbreak of the Spanish war. Following the conflict, it was one of the few items salvaged from the ruins.

"At one point I asked about something to do with politics. His immediate reply was, 'Look, here they'll never ask you about politics. On the other hand, they'll put to you some *bothersome* questions; they'll ask you if you pray, if you use your time well, if you keep your parents happy, if you study, because for a student to study is a grave obligation.' ...'"

After a while the conversation came to a head. "With as much naturalness as directness, Father Josemaría presented me with the following option: 'Of the classes for fellows of your age and studies, there are two that aren't filled yet. Which is better for you?' I chose the second."

Father Escrivá always gave those early classes. "I was impressed," continued Múzquiz, "with the zeal he communicated to the attendants. Even though I belonged to several Catholic youth groups, never had I heard anyone talk the way he did about interior life: prayer, self-denial, the Mass. One could see that he conveyed to us part of his life, something he lived with great intensity."

Within nine months the Academy had outgrown its quarters and was moved to another site, in central Madrid, one that permitted the installation of Opus Dei's first chapel [18]. Father Josemaría was keen on inaugurating the Work's first tabernacle on March 19, the feast of St. Joseph. By mid-March, however, some crucial vessels and vestments had still not been obtained, yet all potential donors had been approached. The founder made a note of what was still needed and showed it to no one but possibly a heavenly friend or two. Just before March 19, a man appeared and entrusted to the doorman a package addressed to Father Escrivá. It contained exactly what was missing. Nothing is known about the donor except that he was bearded.

The second academy, which also featured live-in accommodations, lasted for two years [19]. A resident from Bilbao recalls his impressions:

"There was an extraordinarily pleasant environment of fraternity. We felt very much at home, thanks to the warmth and kindness, shown in a thousand details, that Father Escrivá lived and taught us. I still recall how they cared for me during a slight sickness. To help us keep our priorities straight, Father Escrivá had a parchment prepared for the study room with the words of the New Commandment [20]: 'I give you a new commandment: that you love one another; as I have loved you, so you are to love one another. In this will all men know that you are my disciples, if you have love for one another' (Jn 13:34-35)." This quotation became a traditional feature in all Opus Dei centers for young people, where it is prominently displayed in the study room.

"One essential thing was the cleaning," recalls Pedro Casciaro, another resident. "Since the people hired to do it weren't all that reliable, sometimes we had to do it ourselves. One day when another student and I were leaving later than usual to go to class, we spotted Father Josemaría making a resident's bed and straightening out his room. We immediately joined him, and by following his example I learned the right way to make beds. He taught us to work in God's presence, with order, cheerfulness and good humor."

Every day Father Escrivá crossed half of Madrid to celebrate Mass at St. Elizabeth's, a trip that became more dangerous with each passing day because of frequent attacks on priests by violent anti-clerical gangs. Yet at DYA, residents attest, a feeling of calm prevailed, thanks to the founder's valor. During the summer of 1936 a much larger residence-academy was being set up, only to be abandoned with the start of the Spanish civil war on July 18. There were no distant volleys; the first military clash took place at a barracks across the street from the new center, which was soon a gutted shell.

TRIAL BY WAR

[21] ONCE WASN'T ENOUGH
Close to Madrid was this monumental statue of Christ displaying his sacred heart. The rifles were as real as the virulent anticlericalism of the six militiamen who formed a firing squad for an "execution" during the early months of the civil war. Usually, however, the target was not made of stone; three out of every ten priests in the Madrid diocese were assassinated.

As the shells approached the residence-academy, Father Josemaría heard his followers' confessions before sending them off to find shelter. He did not abandon the building until all had telephoned to say they were safe. Donning a pair of coveralls (till then he was one of the few priests who persisted in wearing the cassock), the founder darted out into the streets awash with the crowds hailing the "Day of Liberation."

Many of the furies released by the war were markedly anticlerical, though persecution of the Church dates from 1931, when the republic was proclaimed. In the various swings of the political pendulum prior to the war, many convents and churches were burned, the Jesuits expelled from the country, Catholic schools banned, and numerous ecclesiastics assaulted, some fatally. When the Popular Front came to power early in 1936, Communists, socialists and anarchists openly prepared for revolution.

When the war exploded, writes historian Andrés Vázquez de Prada, "anticlerical sentiments ran wild, abetted by the authorities. Self-proclaimed militias sprang up to hunt down priests. When clerics were found, they were summarily executed, often at the place of detention." Ecclesiastical records show the death toll: 4,184 diocesan priests and bishops; 2,365 male religious; and 283 female religious (these figures exclude priests or brothers who died in prison or at the front). The diocese of Madrid registered some of the heaviest losses: three out of every ten priests were assassinated [21].

Father Escrivá first found his way to the apartment he shared with his family. But since he was well known in the neighborhood, it was hardly secure. (Some time later, militiamen hanged someone closely resembling Father Escrivá in front of the apartment, probably a case of mistaken identity.) Soon the doorman tipped him off that the building was to be searched for prominent Catholics. He spent the rest of the month hiding here and there. He never wished to stay too

[22] A HUNTED PRIEST
The war found Father Escrivá in Madrid, in the zone soon to be dominated by Communists whose antireligious obsession led them to slay what priests they could find (by the end of the war they had assassinated over 6,000 priests and religious). He doffed his clerical garb and went into hiding, here and there.

Some six weeks into the war, he had taken refuge in an apartment building. One day the militiamen carried out a systematic search, starting in the basement. Alerted, the founder, along with three other refugees, hid in the attic (the interior shown here). Apparently the only door the militiamen did not bother to look behind was this one.

long in any one place, lest his presence endanger his hosts, since sheltering a priest could lead to arrest and even to execution.

August 30 found him hiding in an apartment with several other refugees [22]. One of them had no idea at the time who Father Josemaría was. Years later Juan Manuel Sáinz recalled the moment: "Militiamen had entered the building to carry out a search. They began to comb the basement and then each of the floors.

[23] HIDING AMONG THE INSANE

During the fall and winter of 1936-37, Opus Dei's founder took refuge in the House of Rest and Health (shown here from the back yard), a small residential psychiatric center on the outskirts of Madrid whose director had been a classmate of the founder in Logroño. It housed some 20 patients, a handful of whom, like Father Escrivá, were in hiding. With due caution, while here he made the sacraments available to a number of people and reestablished contact with some of the dispersed members of the Work.

Before they worked their way up to ours, we climbed up to an attic, full of coal dust and junk. The ceiling was too low for us to stand; the heat was unbearable. All this lasted from mid-afternoon till late evening. We heard them enter an adjoining attic. Then Father Josemaría leaned over and whispered, 'I'm a priest; this looks bad; if you wish, make an act of contrition and I'll give you absolution.' But then, for some reason the militiamen didn't bother to search our attic. It was a big risk for him to tell me he was a priest. To save my own life I could have turned him in."

About mid-October arrangements were made for Father Escrivá to go into hiding in a small psychiatric center on the outskirts of Madrid, thanks to the cooperation of its director, Doctor Suils, whom the founder had known in Logroño [23]. For more than four months the House of Rest and Health harbored Opus Dei's founder. With all its risks and inconveniences, it was a relative breathing spell. From that refuge Father Escrivá could reestablish contact with members of the Work. Once he got the lie of the land, he was able to celebrate Mass practically every day. He soon discovered he was not the only one in hiding. He took communion daily to other refugees and trustworthy staff members. To Opus Dei members who visited him there, he would entrust particles of consecrated bread, so they could make communion available to others throughout the beleaguered city.

Those were winter months. Patients suffered from cold as much as hunger. Father Josemaría was given a stove; he in turn gave it to an elderly couple, also in hiding. For two weeks he was left rigid and bedridden by an acute case of rheumatism. Then there was the constant challenge of feigning mental derangement.

He found a somewhat better arrangement, which lasted from March to August, 1937. It was the home of the Honduran Consul General, which enjoyed a precarious diplomatic immunity—enough in any case to protect some 60 refugees. In what was equivalent to a 9-by-12 foot room, Father Escrivá was joined by five other people: four of the Work and his 17-year-old brother Santiago [24]. Though the militia did not always observe the niceties of extraterritoriality, it was better than nothing. "The absence of everything," comments one of the six, "the straits of our confinement, the ever-lurking dangers brought with them a hidden blessing. Without doubt it was Father Escrivá who kept alive in us a determined abandonment in God's hands."

Somewhere they obtained four mattresses and some crates. Their "library" consisted of a few bilingual dictionaries. Their skimpy lunch and supper (no breakfast) usually featured stale carob beans (then equated with animal feed), together with what they called "proteins": a reference to the insects that had gotten to the beans first. As usual, Father Josemaría set up a schedule and assigned chores. That inauspi-

PLANTA DE NUESTRA GALGUERA

[24] PRECARIOUS DIPLOMATIC IMMUNITY

From March to August, 1937, while war still raged throughout the peninsula, Father Escrivá, his brother, and four
Opus Dei members, lived in a small room in an apartment
of the Honduran Consul General in downtown Madrid,
which had attracted over 50 other refugees. Shown is a
drawing of "the layout of our doghouse"—so the title reads
—showing how the approximately 9-by-12 room looked at
night. The drawing was made at the time by Alvaro del
Portillo, one of the occupants, later to be Father Escrivá's
successor. A translation of the numbered objects:

1. Father (Escrivá)
2. Santiago
   (his 17-year-old
   brother)
3. Juan
4. Eduardo
5. José María
6. Alvaro
7. Suitcase with
   Juan's clothing
8. Bench, suitcase and
   clothing of 1 and 2

9. Box, suitcase and
   clothing of José María
10. José María's suitcase
11. Mattress (unused) and
    Eduardo's clothing
12. Radiator, cups,
    holy water and
    tomatoes
13. Alarm clock
14. Door and clothing.

[25] ON THE OUTSIDE AGAIN

After 13 months of war and with no end in sight, Father Josemaría decided to leave the relative safety of the Honduran premises with documentation accrediting him as an employee of the consulate, in order to try to escape to the other side of Spain. There, without the threat of religious persecution, he could take up again the Work's apostolate. While waiting for a chance to leave Madrid, he carried out his priestly ministry in the capital. The photo is from this period, showing the founder in civilian clothes. He slept in an attic; during the day he baptized, said Mass, administered the last rites and heard many confessions, usually while walking in the street. He even conducted an itinerant retreat.

[26] A "WALKING" TABERNACLE

The uppermost object is a cigarette case in which for a time the founder carried about with him particles of the blessed sacrament after abandoning the Honduran refuge. This allowed him to offer communion to persons who had been denied the sacraments for at least a year. The tiny corporal was made for this purpose by his sister Carmen. The canvas bag in which the cigarette case was inserted bears both the flag of Honduras and the seal of its legation in Madrid, where Father Escrivá hid for almost six months.

cious room was to be a home filled with prayer, good cheer and study, with no idleness.

The founder preached daily and celebrated Mass. They also carried out the spiritual practices that had become habitual in Opus Dei (all long traditional in the Church): mental prayer, rosary, spiritual reading, examination of conscience...Time left over was devoted to studying foreign languages and to corresponding with members and friends. Liaison with other members on the outside was maintained by Isidoro Zorzano, who displayed his Argentine citizenship and thus evaded detention. This meant, among other things, that Isidoro would memorize medita-

tions the founder had given to report them verbatim to members in hiding or imprisoned.

Father Escrivá intensified his penance: self-flogging, for example. He ate much less than the others. When his mother made a rare visit to the building, she barely recognized her emaciated son. Above all he suffered for those on the outside deprived of the sacraments and other priestly attentions. It was this concern that led him to quit the Honduran premises on the last day of August, 1937 [25]. The best documentation he could muster was a paper accrediting him as an employee of the consulate.

The next 40 days saw him carry out a vast array of priestly activity: many confessions (usually in the street), Masses in various homes, even a three-day, five-man itinerant retreat (to avoid suspicion and arrest). He sought out and ministered to abandoned groups of nuns. Convinced that his guardian angel was the best of bodyguards, he carried about with him particles of the blessed sacrament in a cigarette case, wrapped in a sheath that bore the flag and seal of the Honduran consulate [26]. "Many times," he later said,

[27] A MISSAL IN THE KNAPSACK

Fall, 1937: Father Josemaría gathered some members of the Work and a few friends in Barcelona in order to attempt to escape to the other half of Spain. With that in mind one of them copied the prayers of the Mass, including texts of the Mass of Mary Mediatrix (shown here), which the founder used before and during the hazardous hike toward independent Andorra, nestled in the Pyrenees Mountains between Spain and France.

[28] A DISGUISE THAT WORKED

Shown is a drawing of Father Josemaría "in the mountains of Rialp" made by Pedro Casciaro, one of his companions during the escape from religious persecution in Spain. The drawing is one of several that illustrated a diary kept by the group. Each of the men was assigned a chore or two to make life a bit less disorderly and unpleasant and to occupy the time—and forestall nerves—whenever the expedition, led by smugglers, had to lie low.

The founder is dressed much like a peasant of the area: with beret, turtle-neck sweater, corduroy pants and field boots.

Padre
en los montes de Rialp

"I slept with my clothes on, with the blessed sacrament wrapped in my arms."

During this time Father Josemaría lived in an attic. He could put up with all kinds of privations, but he missed not having an image of his heavenly mother. To remedy the situation he went to a store. "They were alarmed," he later recounted. "I drew out my documentation, and they very secretly fetched one from deep in storage."

In his comings and goings, Father Escrivá learned of the possibility of escaping from that half of Spain dominated by the Communists via the Pyrenees Mountains and Andorra. Then he could enter the Nationalist zone and establish himself where Catholicism could be practiced. That would also allow him to attend to Opus Dei members and friends fighting on the various battlefronts. On the other hand, he would have to leave behind amid the dangers of Madrid both his natural family and Opus Dei members who could not accompany him. After no little soul-searching, freedom to make his priesthood available to more people won out.

In the fall of 1937 Father Josemaría gathered together four of his followers and two of their friends, most of military age. After many vicissitudes the group established themselves in Barcelona, where they could make contact with the smugglers who would guide them north, through forests and mountains, to the French border. The stay in the Mediterranean port

[29] AN ALTAR IN THE WILDERNESS
On the central rock in this photo Opus Dei's founder celebrated Mass for the last time in the Pyrenees before escaping from religious persecution. Years later one of his companions reconstructed the two-week trek and took this photograph.
Antonio Dalmases, a component of another group that met up with the founder and his companions not long before they reached the border, was an eyewitness to that Mass and recorded in his diary: "...I've never heard Mass like today. I don't know if it's because of the circumstances or because the celebrant is a saint. The communion is moving; we can barely move. We are dressed in rags, dirty and unshaven; our hair needs combing; our bodies, sleep. Our hands are bloodied with scratches, our eyes shine with tears; above all God is with us...."

city lasted more than five trying weeks. The network of underground guides was skittish about taking on new groups. Earlier that fall an expedition of refugees had been seized, and patrols had been beefed up. The group's scant money was running out; falsified documentation was wearing thin. The seven spent most of their time walking to and fro, anywhere, to get in shape for the trek. Father Josemaría continued to lose weight. It was highly doubtful whether he could withstand the rigors of the escape, given the cold, damp fall weather and his physical condition.

The up-and-down, zigzag escape lasted two weeks [27, 28]. They walked by night and hid during daylight. As they drew closer to the frontier, they were joined by other small groups. Father Josemaría made the sacraments available whenever possible [29]. Antonio Dalmases, an eye-witness, committed to his diary an account: "The most moving moment of the trip was the holy Mass: a priest in our company says Mass on a rock. He doesn't say it like the priests in the churches. His clear and heartfelt words penetrate to our souls. I've never heard Mass like today. I don't know if it's because of the circumstances or because the celebrant is a saint. The communion is moving;

we can barely move. We are dressed in rags, dirty and unshaven; our hair needs combing; our bodies, sleep. Our hands are bloodied with scratches, our eyes shine with tears; above all God is with us in the host." Finally, on December 2, 1937, they reached Andorra. The first snowfall of the season, which would have made their detection easier, came unseasonably late — on De-

The exhausted group reached Andorra on December 2, 1937, and remained there for eight days, during which this photo was taken. The first thing Father Escrivá did was to say Mass (in a church for the first time in 17 months); then he sent a postcard to the Consul General of Honduras, back in Madrid.
Of the friends who accompanied the founder in the escape, two had shared with him the attic where they very narrowly avoided arrest shortly after the war began, while another had taken part in an itinerant retreat in Madrid preached by Father Escrivá after leaving the Honduran legation.

cember 4th. After a rest the group then proceeded to France, Lourdes, and Nationalist Spain [30, 31].

Father Josemaría established himself in Burgos, the former capital of Old Castile some 150 miles north of Madrid and the provisional home of Madrid's bishop [32]. For over a year he carried out an intense apostolate, in Burgos and wherever the few pesetas (and lacking those, his prayers) would take him. Later he left a partial account:

"A lot of young men on leave, as well as many who were stationed in the city, came to spend a few days with me. The living quarters that I shared with a few of my sons consisted of a single room in a dilapidated hotel and, though we lacked even the most basic amenities, we organized things in such a way that the men who came—there were hundreds of them—had whatever they needed to rest and recover their strength.

"We used to go for walks along the banks of the Arlanzón River. There we would talk and while they opened their hearts, I tried to guide them with suitable advice to confirm their decisions or open up new horizons in their interior lives. And always, with God's help, I would do all I could to encourage them and stir up in their hearts the desire to live genuinely Christian lives.

"I used to enjoy climbing up the cathedral towers to get a close view of the ornamentation at the top, a veritable lacework of stone that must have been the result of very patient and laborious craftsmanship. As I chatted with the young men who accompanied me I used to point out that none of the beauty of this work could be seen from below. To give them a material lesson in what I had been previously explaining to them, I would say, 'This is God's work, this is

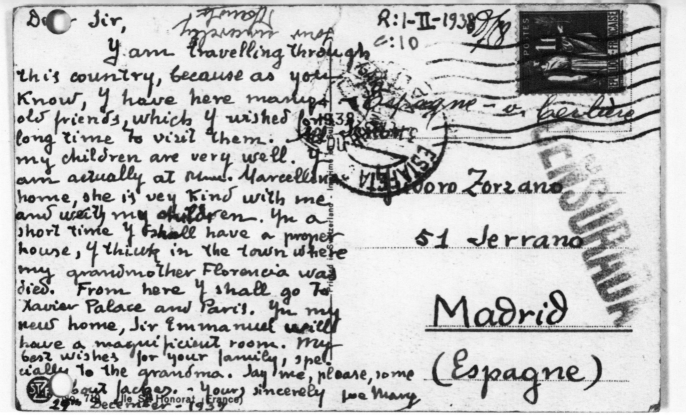

[31] GETTING PAST THE CENSOR

In escaping to the other half of Spain, Father Josemaría had left behind, mostly in Madrid, some members of the Work, his mother, sister and brother. He was eager to let them know of his whereabouts and to keep their hopes alive. Still there was no exchange of mail between Spain's warring sides, and any mail that did get through would be checked by the censors and could not risk any religious references.

By mid-December, 1937, Father Josemaría found himself a guest of the bishop of Pamplona in northern Spain. He could send mail to a friend in southern France, who could remail letters bound for Madrid. By this time also Father Josemaría had developed a vocabulary that could get around censorship, particularly when expressed in a foreign language like English. Thus, the above postcard (stamped "Censored" on the right) he wrote on December 29 to Isidoro Zorzano who, owing to his Argentine citizenship, enjoyed some freedom of movement and continued to serve as liaison among Opus Dei members in Madrid. The postcard's text in faltering English and some explanations follow:

Dear Sir,

I am travelling through this country, because as you know, I have here manys old friends, which I wished for long time to visit them. All my children [those who accompanied him to Andorra] are very well. I am actually at Madame Marcellina's home [the Pamplona bishop's first name was Marcelino], she is very kind with me and with my children. In a short time I shall have a proper [my own] house, I think in the town where my grandmother Florencia was died [Burgos]. From here I shall go to Xavier Palace [an allusion to Vitoria, another Spanish city, where another friend, Javier by name, headed the diocese] and Paris [apparently to throw off the censor]. In my new home, Sir Emmanuel [the Lord] will have a magnificent room [chapel]. My best wishes for your family, specially to the grandma [his mother]. Say me, please, some [news] about Jackes [his brother Santiago]. Yours sincerely, Joe Mary [Josemaría].

working for God!—to finish your personal work perfectly, with all the beauty and exquisite refinement of this tracery stonework.' Seeing it, my companions would understand that all the work we had seen was a prayer, a loving dialogue with God. The men who spent their energies there were quite aware that no one at street level could appreciate their efforts. Their work was for God alone."

The founder resumed his doctoral dissertation in civil law (most of his papers had been lost in the melee of the war). He added to his book *Spiritual Considerations* so that, right after the war, it could be published as *The Way* [54]. He preached many retreats. Above all he renewed contact with all those men, now fighting on various fronts throughout the peninsula, who earlier had found a stimulus and home in Opus Dei. Tomás Alvira, who met Father Escrivá at that itinerant retreat in wartime Madrid, who crossed the Pyrenees with him, and who later was one of the first married members of Opus Dei, has kept one of the founder's many wartime letters. Dated February 4, 1938, it reads:

> May Jesus watch over you.
>
> Dear Tomás,
>   How I would like to be with you. In the meantime, please help us with your prayers and your work.
>   I am trotting all over the place; I am just back from Vitoria and Bilbao. Before that I was in Palencia, Valladolid, Salamanca and Avila. I am just recovering from a cold I caught in the north.
>   Tomás, when can you break away so we can chat?

If the soldiers could not visit Burgos on furlough, he would seek them out, especially if their letters had dried up. Thus did he occupy his time until March,

1939, when the 37-year-old founder was one of the first civilians to enter the newly liberated Madrid.

What was left of the residence-academy from which Father Josemaría had fled when the war started [33]? Combing through the debris, he came across the framed parchment containing the text of the New Commandment [20]. There was no trace, however, of "Our Lady of the Kisses." "I had," he later recalled, "an image of our Lady that the Communists stole from me during the Spanish War. I called it the Virgin of the kisses. I never went in or out of that first residence of ours without first going to the director's room, where the image was, and kissing it. I don't think I ever did it mechanically. It was a human kiss, the kiss of a son who is afraid.... But I have said so often that I am not afraid of anyone or anything, so we'd better not say afraid. It was the kiss of a son who was worried that he was too young and who went to seek in our Lady all the tenderness of her affection. I went to seek all the fortitude I needed in God through the blessed Virgin."

[33] PICKING UP THE POSTWAR PIECES

The Spanish civil war came to an end. Madrid had been taken by the Nationalists on March 28, 1939. That same day Father Escrivá returned to the capital. Below we see him (with his brother Santiago and Juan Jiménez in an officer's uniform) surveying the remains of the second academy-residence. It had received not only the brunt of artillery and bombs; it had also housed a Communist cell. The following October a new residence was opened in Madrid; about the same time the apostolic expansion started with a small center in Valencia. Opus Dei then had about as many members as years had passed since its founding in 1928.

A BUSY DECADE

[34] A ROOM FOR THE FOUNDER
In the new residence in Madrid—three rented floors of a small apartment house—a room was set aside for Father Josemaría, where he worked, sometimes slept (in the primitive sofa-bed on the right) and, above all, talked with the men who sought his spiritual guidance. The photo is from school year 1939-40.

A new residence hall was opened in Madrid in August, 1939 [34, 35]. There Father Escrivá received hundreds of persons who sought his spiritual counsel. He also would travel nearly every weekend to a different Spanish city in search of young men and women who might understand Opus Dei and shape their lives accordingly [36, 37]. Vocations were springing up. To assure them a period of special training, in 1940 he set up what he called a center of studies, where he could live with and train some 20 members of the Work. For all practical purposes, Father Escrivá found he had to begin the women's branch again. He did so with such vigor that they were able to open their first center in 1942 [38].

"I was living in Valencia in 1941," recounts Encarnación Ortega, "when a copy of *The Way* reached my hands. I was deeply impressed. It opened to me the prospect that full-fledged sanctity was not out of the question, and that I could strive for it right where I was."

Shortly thereafter she learned that its author was to give a retreat to young women in Valencia; she signed up, one of several score. "At first we didn't know what to expect, but as soon as we started listening to Father Escrivá, there came over us a deep mood of prayer. When the first session ended, I went to a small reception room to make a courtesy call, just to please my brother. Father Escrivá received me with the amiability that I was later to know as his hallmark. My timidity disappeared. He invited me to come in, instructing me to leave the door open, since that was his custom whenever he received women outside the confessional.

"He immediately began to talk to me about the Work: ordinary Christians, but with a full dedication to serve God...to bring Christ to the summit of all activities, from within the world, without forming ghettos...to reach souls we must go to the very doors of hell....

"I was left with my mouth agape. He said that our Lord wanted all of *that* in the midst of the world, that it had been entrusted to him to make of it a reality, while relying on God's grace. He added that he needed a handful of valiant women, very close to the Virgin, who wanted to be his followers and help him to do this Work of God."

And how did this panorama leave Encarnación? "I didn't feel like eating; I couldn't sleep. I wanted the retreat to end soon so that I might never see this priest again. Still those divine plans he'd shown me kept circulating in my brain. Every time I entered the chapel for a meditation I began to seat myself farther away from the sanctuary. Near the end of the retreat I was sitting in the last pew.

"In the final meditation Father Josemaría spoke about Christ's passion. With great strength he described the Lord's sufferings, from his prayer in the garden to the crucifixion. Having made those scenes come alive, he then added, 'All this—all of it—he has suffered for you. There you have him in the tabernacle. At least have the nobility to look him in the face and say to him, "*That* which you are asking of me, I don't want to give to you".'

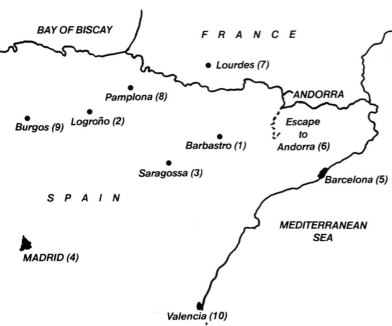

Shown are many of the sites that figure in the story of Opus Dei's founder up through 1939. (1) Barbastro, in Aragon, was his mother's hometown and home for the Escrivás from 1898 to 1915, during which Josemaría was born; nearby lies the shrine of Our Lady of Torreciudad. (2) Logroño was home for the Escrivá family from 1915 to 1925; here José died. (3) Josemaría was ordained in Saragossa, after four years at St. Francis Seminary; for two more years the young priest lived here, as did his mother, sister and brother.

(4) A year before Opus Dei was born, Father Josemaría moved to the capital, where he remained till 1937. (5) Midway through the civil war the founder spent some time in Barcelona in preparation for the escape from religious persecution. (6) The broken line traces the route that Father Josemaría and his companions followed in making their way on foot through the Pyrenees Mountains to Andorra. They had taken a bus from Barcelona, and to avoid detection had gotten off at various points along the way, finally assembling to begin the trek. (7) After reaching Andorra, they wended their way through France to the southwest corner where they entered Nationalist Spain, after a stop at the shrine in Lourdes to thank God's Mother for her protection.

(8) Pamplona is where Father Josemaría rested as a guest of the archbishop for a while after the escape; the Navarrese capital is today the home of the University of Navarre, founded by Monsignor Escrivá. (9) Early in 1938 the founder made his way to Burgos, provisional home of Madrid's bishop, and from there he reorganized the apostolate. (10) Shortly after the war and once more established in Madrid, the founder visited, among other cities, Valencia, where a small center of Opus Dei was opened in the fall of 1939, the start of the expansion.

"In that very moment I fully resolved to answer Yes: I was willing to be one of the women alongside our sorrowful Mother who were willing to help Father Escrivá bring about Opus Dei in the world. As soon as I told him, he helped me to see that I would encounter difficulties and the demands of dedication: there was still no center where his daughters could live...people might not understand our way...ours would be real poverty: I had to be ready to forsake my possessions and dreams about the future. I also had to be available to go wherever needed and, if required, to learn other languages to be able to work in France, England, Japan or other countries.... Doubtless Father Escrivá's prayer made it possible for me to see all of that as feasible."

While those early members were the apple of his eye, Father Escrivá somehow found time to attend to the requests of bishops from all corners of Spain to preach retreats to their clergy. Even 40 years later participants could still recall his message. While he was away from Madrid on one of those retreats in 1941, his mother died quite unexpectedly, after having helped her son for years to make of Opus Dei a family and a home [1].

Back in Madrid, tears coursing down his cheeks, the son could not contain his grief: "My God, my God, what have you done? You're taking everything away from me...everything. I thought my mother was needed by these daughters of mine, and you leave me with nothing...nothing at all."

Amid all this, a fierce persecution—not the last—was to break out: a mixture of misunderstandings, calumnies and jealousy. Some priests and religious took the lead. Opus Dei and its founder were denounced, even from the pulpit. *The Way* was publicly burned. Parents of students in contact with Opus Dei were warned about this "heretic." In Barcelona a warrant for his arrest was issued. Lest they fail to live justice or charity, Father Josemaría forbade members even to mention these painful events.

From the start Opus Dei enjoyed the approval and encouragement of Madrid's bishop (later archbishop). Throughout these trials the prelate staunchly defended God's Work. To put an end to the persecution, he convinced the founder that it should be formally approved, at least temporarily, as a Pious Union. That took place in 1941, but did not succeed in quieting Opus Dei's enemies.

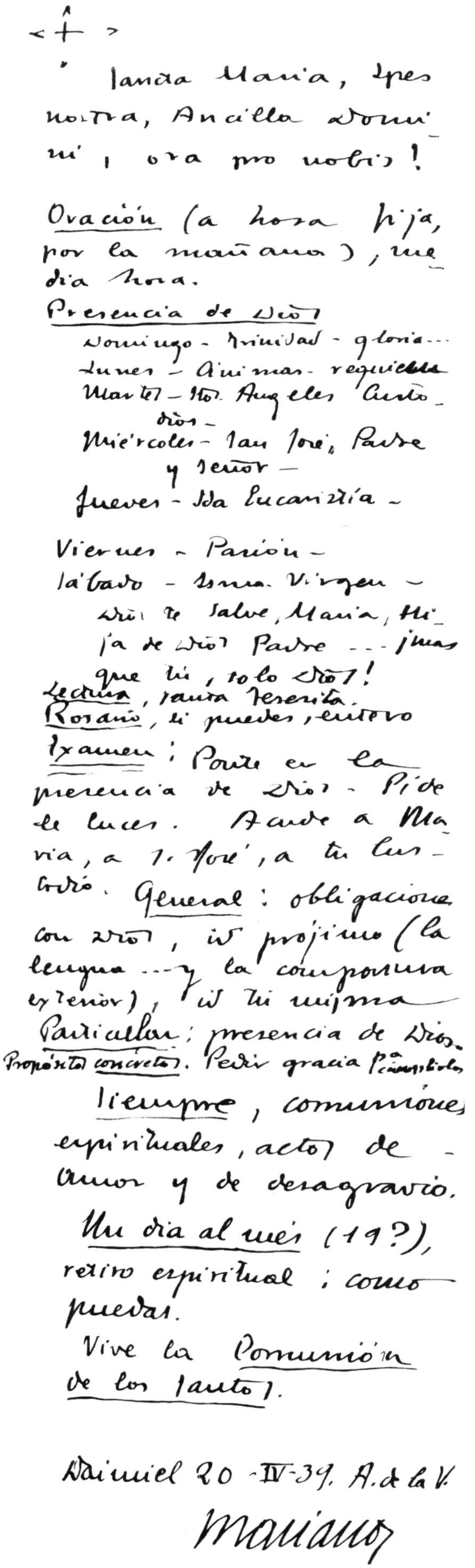

handwritten Spanish manuscript in left column

⟨✝⟩

Sancta María, Spes
nostra, Ancilla Domi-
ni, ora pro nobis!

Oración (a hora fija,
por la mañana), media
día hora.
Presencia de Dios
  Domingo – Trinidad – gloria…
  Lunes – Ánimas – requiem
  Martes – Stos. Ángeles Custo-
    dios –
  Miércoles – San José, Padre
    y Señor –
  Jueves – Sda. Eucaristía –

  Viernes – Pasión –
  Sábado – Sma. Virgen –
    Dios te salve, María, Hi-
    ja de Dios Padre … Más
    que tú, solo Dios!
Lectura, santa Teresita.
Rosario, si puedes, entero
Examen: Ponte en la
presencia de Dios. Pide
le luces. Acude a Ma-
ría, a S. José, a tu Cus-
todio. General: obligaciones
con Dios, iù prójimo (la
lengua … y la compostura
exterior), iù ti misma
Particular: presencia de Dios.
Propósitos concretos. Pedir gracia p cumplirlos
  Siempre, comuniones
espirituales, actos de
amor y de desagravio.
  Un día al mes (19?),
retiro espiritual; como
puedas.
  Vive la Comunión
de los santos.

Daimiel 20 - IV - 39. A. d la V.

Mariano

[36] LESS THAN THREE WEEKS AFTER THE WAR

During the war Father Escrivá had corresponded with the Fisac family in the town of Daimiel, some hundred miles south of Madrid. His correspondent was Lola, whose brother had been in contact with the Work before the war, went into hiding and relied on his sister for communication.

On returning to Madrid as the war concluded, Father Escrivá found that, for all practical purposes, he would have to begin again his apostolic work with women. He remembered Lola and made it to Daimiel less than three weeks after the hostilities ceased. They talked, and she reaffirmed her desire to join Opus Dei. For starters, the founder explained to her a program of prayer, which he also wrote out on three sheets (shown here). A translation:

Holy Mary, our hope, handmaid of the Lord, pray for us!

Prayer (at a fixed time, in the morning), half an hour.
Presence of God
  Sunday—Trinity—Gloria…
  Monday—souls in purgatory—requiem
  Tuesday—holy guardian angels
  Wednesday—St. Joseph, father and lord
  Thursday—holy Eucharist
  Friday—passion
  Saturday—most holy Virgin
    Hail Mary, daughter of God the Father…, greater than you only God!
Reading, [book of] St. Teresita [Thérèse of Lisieux]
Rosary, if you can, all of it
Examination: Put yourself in the presence of God. Ask for light. Turn to Mary, St. Joseph, your guardian angel.
  General: duties toward God, toward your neighbor (the tongue…your bearing), toward yourself
  Particular [exam]: presence of God
Specific resolutions. Ask for grace to fulfill them.
Always, spiritual communions, acts of love and of reparation
One day a month (19th?), a day of recollection: as best you can.
Live the *Communion of the saints*.

(It is signed "Mariano," one of his baptismal names, which, with the occasion of the war, he started to use owing in part to his devotion to Mary.) Father Escrivá also asked her to write every 8-10 days. He omits any mention of Mass or confession, because churches remained closed in Daimiel and surviving priests were few and far between.

[37] VALLADOLID, SPAIN—MAY, 1940

Valladolid was no longer the capital city of the Empire of Philip II. But it was a university town and relatively close to Madrid: some 100 miles to the northwest. Even before the war ended, the founder visited it and began to meet people and gather names. Towards the end of 1939 he started to visit it again, giving rise to what were soon to become visits every weekend. At first he would go with one or two others and take a room in a hotel, making whatever appointments they could with collegians. When these came in ones or twos, the founder would talk with them and then send them out to bring others. Towards the end of the day the hotel room would be full of both "recruiters" and "recruits." The following weekend, the same. Soon those members who accompanied the founder on the initial trips learned the ropes, and he could absent himself for a while to start the process in another university town.

Of the many students thus met, some discovered their vocation to Opus Dei. The following spring a small apartment, soon dubbed "The Corner," was rented. There the camera found Opus Dei's founder in May 1940.

That same year the Benedictine abbot of Montserrat had written the bishop to inquire about the Work. "I'm aware of the storm," the answer reads in part, "that has been raised in Barcelona against Opus Dei. What is sad is that persons dedicated to God serve as an instrument of evil; of course, *putantes se obsequium praestare Deo* [thinking that they are serving God].... Believe me, Father Abbot, the Opus is truly Dei, from its very conception and in each of its steps and undertakings."

Meanwhile Father Josemaría had other matters to claim his attention. Before the civil war he had had mixed experience in enlisting the help of other diocesan priests to tend to Opus Dei's various apostolates. Somehow Opus Dei would have to have its own priests, schooled in its own lay spirituality, and these would have to come from among its still thin lay ranks.

[38] A HOME FOR OPUS DEI'S WOMEN

Shown is the first center of the women's branch of Opus Dei, opened in 1942 in a quiet residential neighorhood in Madrid. While a few members lived there, above all it was a home for the growing spiritual and apostolic activities they carried out for young women.

Also shown is the interior of the center's chapel. Here Father Escrivá was celebrating Mass in 1943 on the anniversary of the founding of the women's branch, when he saw how Opus Dei might have its own priests. Thus was born the Priestly Society of the Holy Cross.

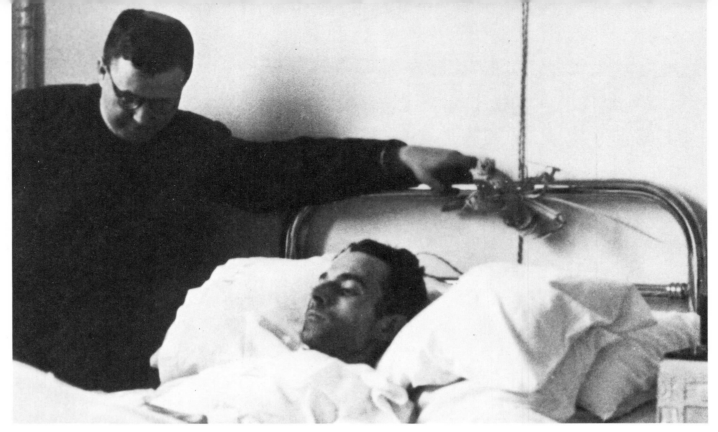

[39] DEATH OF THE OLDEST MEMBER

Father Josemaría is shown at the bedside of Isidoro Zorzano shortly before his death in 1943 at age 41 from Hodgkin's disease. Josemaría and Isidoro had been high school classmates in Logroño. The former went on to the seminary, while the latter studied engineering. They corresponded intermittently. Their paths crossed again in Madrid in 1930, whereupon Isidoro joined the Work. For the next six years professional work kept him in Málaga, except for monthly "escapes" to Madrid on weekends. On the eve of the Spanish war, quite coincidentally, he was transferred to Madrid to work for another Spanish railroad. Since he was born in Argentina before his family moved back to Spain, he enjoyed Argentine citizenship, which excused him from conscription and allowed him a relative freedom of movement in Madrid during the war. In 1948 the process of beatification and canonization of this early member of Opus Dei was opened.

While the founder sought the right canonical formula for these prospective priests, three members, all of whom happened to be engineers, had begun to study for the priesthood. The solution came to Father Escrivá in 1943 while celebrating Mass on the anniversary of the founding of the women's branch. Thus was born the Priestly Society of the Holy Cross. It would consist of members ordained as priests largely to serve Opus Dei's apostolates. This new configuration met the Holy See's requirements in the fall of that year. In June, 1944, after intensive studies and painstaking preparation, the first three priests of Opus Dei were ordained [40].

One of these was Alvaro del Portillo, who had joined the Work before the Spanish war. The man who became Father Escrivá's successor was seldom far from his side, serving as his confessor, his adviser, his right-hand man. (Another of that trio was Father Joseph Múzquiz, who brought the Work to the United States in 1949.)

As the decade progressed, Father Josemaría was winning the "battle of formation," by which he meant preparing members to live Opus Dei's spirit and to

[40] THE FIRST THREE PRIESTS

Until June 25, 1944, Father Escrivá was Opus Dei's only priest. On that date three veteran members of the Work, who since the civil war had worked as engineers in addition to assuming a growing role in its apostolate, were ordained as priests. In the top photo, taken shortly before their ordination, they flank the founder; from left they are José Luis Múzquiz, who helped start Opus Dei in the United States in 1949 and was known as Father Joseph; José María Hernández de Garnica, who worked apostolically in many countries of Europe; and Alvaro del Portillo, even then the founder's right-hand man.

The ceremony took place in the bishop's chapel. In the middle photo the new priests kneel before the ordaining minister, Bishop Leopoldo Eijo y Garay, Madrid's prelate since Opus Dei was founded.

In the bottom photo the bishop, accompanied by Father Escrivá, visits the Moncloa Residence, a larger university residence hall in Madrid opened in 1943. The picture was taken just before the residence's second year of operation.

assume the task of transmitting it to other members and non-members alike, as priests or laymen. "Older" members had taken over the classes in Christian living that Father Josemaría had been giving for so many years. With prepared manpower new centers were opened. The few priests were busy saying Mass, preaching and, more than anything, making themselves available for confession and spiritual guidance.

With mature members the Work could also spread. Just as the Spanish civil war had forced the postponement of plans to open new centers in Valencia and Paris, the Second World War put a temporary halt to expansion beyond Spain. By 1945, however, nine major Spanish cities had Opus Dei centers alongside their universities. In 1946 Father Josemaría sent some of his more experienced sons to start the Work in Portugal, England and Italy. The following year it spread to France and Ireland.

Now that Opus Dei was beginning to be international in fact, it needed more than ever the approval of the Holy See. To that end the founder sent Alvaro del Portillo—first as a layman, then in 1946 as a priest—to Rome to lay the case before officials of the Roman Curia. The reception was mixed. Opus Dei's novel approach to apostolate and its distinctive spirituality met in part with admiration, notably from Monsignor Montini, later Pope Paul VI [42]. Others were skeptical about finding an adequate place for Opus Dei within the Church's structure. In fact a churchman told del Portillo that Opus Dei had been born a century too soon. The emissary wrote back to Madrid saying that only Father Josemaría's presence in Rome could wrench loose a satisfactory solution.

Despite a severe case of diabetes that led his doctors to dissuade him, Opus Dei's founder spent most of the second half of 1946 in Rome, dealing with Vatican officials [41]. Over the next three years Opus Dei received all the Holy See's approvals, though the resulting juridical framework was not quite what its founder had in mind.* Meanwhile Father Escrivá was also named a monsignor.

In the late '40s Opus Dei began to welcome married members. They and the founder had been awaiting

*Early in 1947 Pope Pius XII established a new canonical framework within which Opus Dei could accommodate itself. This legal mold—though it provided a basis for complete Vatican approval of Opus Dei, which was granted in 1950—was not fully suitable. Not until the end of 1982 was Opus Dei made a personal prelature, a new juridical configuration that fully and definitively recognized the Work's characteristics. Almost from the beginning this framework had been conceived and sought by Opus Dei's founder. It was not until Vatican Council II, however, that this canonical option became available. And nearly 20 more years had to pass before Opus Dei became the Church's first personal prelature [68].

[41] TO SEEK THE APPROVAL OF PETER
This small balcony affords a view of the cupola of St. Peter's Basilica in Rome and the adjoining papal apartments. Here in prayer for the Church and Pope Pius XII, Opus Dei's founder spent his first night in Rome in June, 1946. He had come to seek full juridical approval from the Holy See for the novel Catholic organization.

[42] A LONG-TIME FRIEND
The date on the photo reads "Pentecost, 1947." It is signed by Monsignor Giovanni Battista Montini, then the Vatican's Undersecretary of State for ordinary affairs, and later (in 1963) to be Pope Paul VI. The text says, "To the illustrious and reverend Monsignor José María Escrivá de Balaguer y Albás with every best wish for himself and his undertaking." A year earlier the Undersecretary had been one of the first curial officials to take an interest in Opus Dei. "The first affectionate word for the Work heard in Rome was said by him," the founder said.

All'Ill.mo e Rev.mo Mons. José Maria Escrivá
de Balaguer y Albás con ogni miglior
augurio per lui e per il suo lavoro

Pentecoste 1947

G.B. Montini

this moment from the start. Thus began a mobilization that would lead thousands of persons to ratify the vocational dimension of marriage and to assume the task of sanctifying their family life, while converting their dwellings into "bright and cheerful homes," as the founder liked to say. He also stressed that, while their family ties might limit their involvement in Opus Dei as an organization, they had the same contemplative and apostolic vocation as the members called to celibacy.

Opus Dei's founder had always cared deeply for his fellow diocesan priests, helping them to live fully their vocation and ministry. So much so that, with the encouragement of the Holy See, he was willing to found a new association for them and, if necessary, to give up his own involvement in Opus Dei. While wrestling with this question in the years following World War II, he came to see more clearly—as did the See of Peter—that they could be associated with Opus Dei. Lay members did not change their status nor modify their rights and responsibilities by affiliating themselves with Opus Dei. Neither would diocesan priests: they would remain subject to their bishop and continue to carry out their assigned pastoral tasks. Opus Dei offered its lay members help in their spiritual life and apostolate. It would do the same with diocesan priests. This could be accomplished through the Priestly Society of the Holy Cross.

Married persons, diocesan priests...Opus Dei was opening its doors wide—and still wider. From the start, as we have seen, Father Josemaría had sought the help —prayers, penance, alms and services—of many persons who were not themselves called to Opus Dei. Some were not Catholics, not even Christians. This collaboration, while benefiting Opus Dei, mainly redounded to the spiritual welfare of these benefactors, to whom Opus Dei also made available its means of spiritual growth. While the Work had a "single pot," as its founder used to say, assorted people could dip

[43] A CORNERSTONE FOR THE U.S.
Shown is the painting of the blessed Virgin that in 1949 Father Josemaría entrusted to Father Joseph Múzquiz and Sal Ferigle (a physicist later ordained a priest) when they set out from Spain to begin Opus Dei in the United States. In those early days it presided over the chapel of Woodlawn Residence in Chicago. Originally it hung in the hotel room in Burgos where Opus Dei's founder lived in 1938-39. It was later moved to the chapel of the first postwar residence in Madrid, which, thanks to the eagerness of Opus Dei's founder, opened in the fall of 1939.

in their ladles to different depths. With the approval that came in 1950, all these helpers could associate themselves with Opus Dei as cooperators—the first time in the Church's history that non-Catholics could find such a welcome within a Catholic organization.

Opus Dei was born to play a worldwide role. And what better way to foster this universality than alongside the Roman Pontiff? "We have come to serve the Church as the Church wishes to be served," Monsignor Escrivá taught. Not surprisingly, as the 1940s came to a close, Opus Dei established its headquarters in Rome in what was to become a handsome complex of buildings. For ten years the founder faced the weekly crisis of meeting the construction workers' payroll.

But first, an existing building had to be purchased. During the negotiations, Father Escrivá was informed that the owner demanded payment in Swiss francs. His reaction: "Since we don't have a cent, the Lord can as easily give us Swiss francs as Italian liras." One day the former owner paid a visit to what was soon dubbed Villa Tevere. "I see you've changed the floor," he commented. "No, it's the same one—it's been scrubbed."

During these early years the headquarters complex also housed, in separate units, the Roman College of the Holy Cross (for men) and the Roman College of Saint Mary (for women). To them came members from various countries to school themselves in the Work's spirit and traditions and to further their doctrinal education. After several years in Rome, they would return to their native lands—or to a new one— "to do Opus Dei, being yourself Opus Dei," as the founder often said. From their ranks would come also most of the new priests of Opus Dei. The number ordained each year was increasing.

By early 1949 the Work of God was sending down roots in Mexico and the United States [43]. In the following year work began in Argentina and Chile. In most cases, about a year after the men's branch would establish itself, the women's branch would follow. That was some feat, since these women had opened their first center only in 1942.

As time went on, Opus Dei women were entering all the major professions and running the same apostolates as the men. But the "apostolate of apostolates"— the phrase is the founder's—was reserved for the women's branch, and then for only some of them. Throughout the decade specially trained women members had been assuming the domestic tasks in centers of both branches: professionalizing a myriad of housekeeping responsibilities so that the Work's centers were truly family homes.

"How many times did I hear him say," says an early member, "that we ought to kiss our apron, showing thereby our holy pride in carrying out such a noble task?" Monsignor Escrivá took a direct hand in launching this domestic service. "To make meals appetizing and healthy," he would tell them, "is nothing short of a science, even if you can't spend much because we're poor. That's why I've told you that your pantry is a studio and your kitchen a laboratory."

Another early member devoted to domestic work says, "He insisted on our varying the menus and dressing up the food. He recommended cookbooks and culinary magazines. He would often pass along recipes and tips on how to prepare food better. He always concerned himself with our having the necessary appliances, which cut down on personnel, time and, ultimately, money. Those devices also helped us to do a better job."

THE ROMAN YEARS

In 1940 Father Escrivá had been single-handedly directing all the activities of Opus Dei. Ten years later, thanks to his foresight and determination to make Opus Dei universal and permanent, he was able to realize in a new way his dream: "to do and disappear, so that only Christ might shine." For the next two decades he seldom left the Eternal City.

There were times, however, when Monsignor Escrivá's confinement was not fully of his own choosing. In 1944, at El Escorial monastery in Spain, the founder preached a retreat to some hundred Augustinians, despite a fever of 102 degrees. At its conclusion the diagnosis was clear: diabetes mellitus. Even with a vigorous diet and insulin injections, the disorder wreaked havoc on his body: obesity, impaired vision, inflammations, hemorrhaging, a thirst that was as constant as his headache. Except when he was bedridden, those who lived with him in Rome were kept in the dark about his sufferings—all but his confessor, Father del Portillo, and his physician, Doctor Faelli, a Roman specialist in diabetes, who claimed he never saw a worse case.

This was not the first time Opus Dei's founder stayed the course in the face of illness or exhaustion. "In the Work," he would say, "we cannot allow ourselves the luxury of being sick, and I usually ask the Lord to keep me healthy to be able to work for God. Therefore, you have to take care of yourselves, so as to be able to die old, very old, squeezed out like a lemon, accepting from this moment on whatever God has willed for you."

After a decade of physical trials, God apparently altered the course he had laid out for Monsignor Escrivá. One April afternoon in 1954, after entering into a death-like shock brought on, it seems, by modified insulin treatment, the founder awoke cured.

Opus Dei's founder was keen on finishing his job of laying as firm a foundation as possible. That meant, among other things, committing his insights, dispositions and exhortations to paper; gathering and digesting experiences from the field; setting ever higher, broader goals of apostolate for members; directing the worldwide expansion of the Work; and making sure that in everything to do with worship no means were spared in expressing devotion to Jesus Christ and his Mother. Most especially it meant forming his disciples—"my only monuments will be you"—as a good father would, so they could take over the family business, in this case a strictly spiritual enterprise. In essence, that is the outline of what the still "calm whirlwind" set out to accomplish during his Roman enclosure.

There is more to his Roman years than meets the eye. In fact, this new phase would seem to have a lot to do with what Opus Dei is all about: invigorating lay people to assume their full role. In 1932 Father Escrivá wrote down what had been his teaching for at least four years: "The prejudice that ordinary members of the faithful must limit themselves to helping the clergy in ecclesiastical apostolates has to be rejected. There is no reason why the secular apostolate should always be a mere participation in the apostolate of the hierarchy. Secular people too have a duty to carry out the apostolate—not because they receive a canonical mission, but because they are part of the Church. Their mission...is fulfilled in their profession, their job, their family, and among their colleagues and friends."

If lay people did all they could, in the founder's view, then clerics would be less tempted to go beyond their specific mission and take on tasks laymen should bear. This is what Monsignor Escrivá called "a healthy anticlericalism." Thus did he resist unenlightened attempts on the part of the clergy to ape laymen or clericalize them, just as he resisted lay efforts to ape the clergy or secularize them. If cleric and layman alike tried to identify themselves with Christ, then the distinctive apostolic role of each would be clarified

[44] IN ROME AND ON THE HIGHWAYS

December, 1955: the founder stands on the bank of the Rhine River, near Bonn, West Germany, with two members of the Work. Three years earlier Opus Dei had begun to put down roots in that country, and on this brief trip the founder wanted not only to encourage the pioneers, but also to ready the ground in other countries through which he passed. That spadework consisted mainly of prayer, visits to Marian shrines and meetings with ecclesiastical authorities. By then Opus Dei was at work in 16 countries of Europe and North and South America; membership had reached several thousand.

The preceding six years had seen the founder named a monsignor and the Work's headquarters established in Rome. The first married members and diocesan priests (in the Priestly Society of the Holy Cross) had been admitted, the Work had observed its silver anniversary (in 1953), and the founder had been cured of diabetes, the ailment that plagued him for a decade.

[45] 'AUNT' CARMEN IN ROME

Carmen Escrivá, the founder's sister, is shown in her Roman home with Chato, her bulldog, at Christmas, 1956. She had come to Rome four years earlier to lend yet another hand. "It was very good for us," acknowledged Monsignor Escrivá, "that my mother and my sister Carmen willingly took over the housekeeping chores in our first centers....If not, we would not have had a true home: it would have turned out to be some kind of barracks."

Members of the Work spontaneously took to calling her aunt, and not only because she was the founder's sister. She remembered not only the early members' names, but their favorite dishes, desserts and candies; she noticed when a button was about to fall and would activate her expert needle....

This was to be her last Christmas: she died of cancer the following June.

and complemented.

Monsignor Escrivá saw himself called not only to help the laity discover their mission, but also to help clerics work within theirs. In an interview he said as much:

"Alongside the laity's new awareness of their role, there is a similar development among the clergy. They too are coming to realize that lay people have a role of their own, which should be fostered and stimulated by pastoral action aimed at discovering in the midst of the People of God the charisms of holiness and apostolate. This new pastoral approach, though very demanding, is, to my mind, absolutely necessary....I feel we priests are being asked to have the humility of learning not to be fashionable, of being in fact servants of the servants of God and making our own the cry of the Baptist: 'He must increase; I must decrease,' so as to enable ordinary Christians, the laity, to make Christ present in all sectors of society."

Throughout the fifties and sixties, members of Opus Dei were sent to a host of new countries with the founder's blessing, an image of the blessed Virgin and little or nothing else. There each took up again his professional task. In 1951 they went to Venezuela and Colombia; in 1952, Germany; 1953, Peru and Guatemala; 1954, Ecuador; 1956, Uruguay and Switzerland; 1957, Brazil, Austria and Canada; 1958, El Salvador, Kenya and Japan; 1959, Costa Rica. In 1960 it was to Holland; 1962, Paraguay; 1963, Australia; 1964, the Philippines; 1965, Nigeria and Belgium; and in, 1969,

[46] SUMMERS IN ENGLAND

Monsignor Escrivá spent at least part of each summer in England from 1958 to 1962. Here we see him outside the Church of St. Dunstan with Father del Portillo (on the left) and Father Javier Echevarría, his longtime aides. St. Dunstan's, in Canterbury, contains the head of St. Thomas More, to whom the founder was devoted. Opus Dei's founder, like St. Thomas a lawyer, visited the shrine several times.

During that first summer he manifested a great apostolic interest in Oxford University, which soon led, not without some difficulties, to the conversion of Grandpont House, near the campus, into a center of Opus Dei. By 1959 he also got his wish to have a relic of Thomas More: a piece of the hairshirt the Renaissance scholar, family man and Lord Chancellor wore until his beheading.

Puerto Rico. . . .

To say Monsignor Escrivá alternated work and prayer is only a half-truth. For many years now he claimed that his work had become another form of contemplation, just as his prayer was productive of deeds. He strove to work always in union with God. Mentally, if not physically, he would often go to the tabernacle, never far away.

The founder's meals were plain, when not frugal. He always tried to set aside some time each day to receive visitors. His warmth and intensity were such that many came away from their brief encounters thinking, as an American author, Daniel Sargent, wrote in his

"We have filled the highways of Europe with Hail Marys and songs," said the founder. Here he is shown in 1960 kissing the wall of the grotto at Lourdes, which he had first visited in 1937, after escaping from religious persecution in Spain. There is hardly a Marian shrine in western Europe that Monsignor Escrivá did not visit in private pilgrimages in the last three decades of his life. He would combine them with trips to countries where Opus Dei members were starting or expanding—or would shortly begin.

was so warm, cheerful, even playful, while no less spiritual and demanding. We loved to be with him, even if for just a few moments. We'd drop anything and rush to hear him talk. About what? 'Only about God', as he put it—and did. But his was no dry sermonizing. That smile and especially those twinkling eyes betrayed a man in love, out to spread his good fortune.

"I sometimes wondered afterwards what defects, if any, our founder might have had. I had heard him on numerous occasions take exception to the tendency in biographies of saints to describe them as though sanctity came easy to them. He himself had written, 'The true life stories of Christian heroes resemble our own experiences: they fought and won; they fought and lost. And then, repentant, they returned to the fray.' Monsignor Escrivá did have a temper. He himself said on more than one occasion: 'Sometimes I get angry because I should, at other times because I'm a poor man.' His anger was never without cause nor did it leave a bad taste. An apology usually followed upon any display of displeasure."

If Monsignor Escrivá had a forceful personality, it was in the service of his mission. Those who dealt with him were usually surprised at the depth of his humility. He was a keen listener, ever ready to learn. If he found he had come to a decision on the basis of insufficient data, he was quick to rectify mistakes, often publicly. He would greet the slightest favor with uncommon gratitude. He was unassuming and spontaneous. He made holiness humanly attractive. As he often said, "We have to be very human; otherwise we cannot be divine."

By 1950 or so, the basic elements of the Work's structure and spirit were all in place. During the next 25 years the founder was to spend most of his time tending to the expansion and consolidation of Opus Dei, largely from Rome. He was determined to see

diary, "Today I have met a saint." Monsignor Escrivá preached often; he wrote a great deal, largely in the form of longer letters to Opus Dei members that showed the concern of a good shepherd.

Twice a day he would gather with others for a brief get-together, long an Opus Dei tradition. This was a time for simple and affectionate family life: sharing news, commenting on events, recounting apostolic episodes, maybe an occasional song or joke. Sometimes the founder would bare his heart or answer questions with the desire of helping his spiritual children to be more united to God and of greater service to their fellow men.

"It's difficult to describe," admits John Coverdale, an early American member, referring to the years he spent in close proximity to Monsignor Escrivá. "He

[48] WITH 'THE SWEET CHRIST ON EARTH'

Monsignor Escrivá made his own this phrase that St. Catherine of Siena sometimes used to refer to the Roman Pontiff. Shown are the founder and Father del Portillo with Pope John XXIII, who entrusted to Opus Dei a large social-educational-apostolic undertaking, later blessed by Paul VI, in a section of Rome known as "little Moscow."

This devotion to the Pope—"whoever he is"—was a mainstay of the founder, who said, "When you are old, and I have already rendered my account to God, you will tell...how the Father loved the Pope with all his soul, with all his strength."

Before and during Vatican Council II, he made fully available Opus Dei's secretary general, Alvaro del Portillo, for service on many commissions, notably as Secretary to the one dealing with "the discipline of the clergy and Christian people."

Many conciliar participants saw in the founder a "precursor" of the essential teachings of Vatican II. The Council echoed his pioneering efforts when it declared, for example: "The apostolate of the laity is a sharing in the salvific mission of the Church. Through Baptism and Confirmation all are appointed to this apostolate by the Lord himself. Moreover, by the sacraments, and especially by the Eucharist, that love of God and man which is the soul of the apostolate is communicated and nourished. The laity, however, are given this special vocation: to make the Church present and fruitful in those places and circumstances where it is only through them that she can become the salt of the earth. Thus, every lay person, through those gifts given to him, is at once the witness and the living instrument of the mission of the Church herself 'according to the measure of Christ's bestowal'."

[49] THE UNIVERSITY OF NAVARRE

In 1952, backed by the founder's prayers and encouragement, some members of Opus Dei, all professors, started what was to become, eight years later, the University of Navarre in Pamplona, Spain—the first of many initiatives in higher education (others are in Mexico, Peru, Colombia, Kenya, Japan, the Philippines...). The camera shows Monsignor Escrivá surrounded by students in Pamplona in 1960, the year the new university was inaugurated.

[50] 'PASSIONATELY LOVING THE WORLD'

Such was the title and thrust of a homily given by Monsignor Escrivá to over 40,000 persons during an open-air Mass celebrated on the campus of the University of Navarre in October, 1967. The founder is shown with a youthful participant. In many ways that homily sounds like a *Magna Carta* of the laity; some excerpts:

"...Everyday life is the true setting for your lives as Christians. Your ordinary contact with God takes place where your fellow men, your yearnings, your work and your affections are. There you have your daily encounter with Christ. It is in the midst of the most material things of the earth that we must sanctify ourselves, serving God and all mankind.... Have not doubt: any kind of evasion from the honest realities of daily life is for you, men and women of the world, something opposed to God's will....

"We cannot lead a double life. We cannot be like schizophrenics if we want to be Christians. There is just one life, made of flesh and spirit. And it is this life that has to become, in both soul and body, holy and filled with God.

...Either we learn to find our Lord in ordinary, everyday life, or else we shall never find him. That is why I can tell you that our age needs to give back to matter and to the most trivial occurrences and situations their noble and original meaning. It needs to restore them to the service of the Kingdom of God, to spiritualize them, turning them into a means and an occasion for a continuous meeting with Jesus Christ....

"That is why I have told you repeatedly, and hammered away once and again on the idea, that the Christian vocation consists in making heroic verse out of the prose of each day. Heaven and earth seem to merge, my children, on the horizon. But where they really meet is in your hearts, when you sanctify your everyday lives...."

[51] FIRST VISIT TO THE AMERICAS

Monsignor Escrivá had an established history of taking all his concerns for the Church to the blessed Virgin. In 1970 a pilgrimage to the shrine at Fatima was not enough for him. He continued westward in a first trip to the new world, to Mexico City, where he made a novena—several hours a day—before the revered image of Our Lady of Guadalupe. That first visit was to last 40 days, during which he saw tens of thousands of Opus Dei's "extended family" in cordial question-and-answer gatherings. The format served to stir the faith and practice of all kinds of people.

We see him with a group of Mexican farmers. Among other things, he told them: "You and we, all of us, are concerned that you improve, that you rise above this situation, so you no longer have financial pressures….(Referring to a school set up by members of Opus Dei) We are also going to try to help your children get an education: you'll see how among all of us we'll achieve it and that those who have the talent and desire to study go very far. At the beginning they'll be few, but with the years… And how will we do it? Like someone doing a favor? No, not at all, my children. Haven't I told you that we are all equals?"

To those in a position to help the disadvantaged, he insisted: "We have to do more for workers and peasants. We have to help them, with human warmth and supernatural affection, to learn whatever is necessary for them to draw a greater material yield from their work and thus to maintain their families with greater ease and dignity. For that we don't have to pull down those who are on top, but neither is it just that there be families that stay always on the bottom. …My children, I'm not speaking about charities or beneficence. Charity we have in our hearts; to provide material means is a duty for those who have received them from God so as to be their administrators."

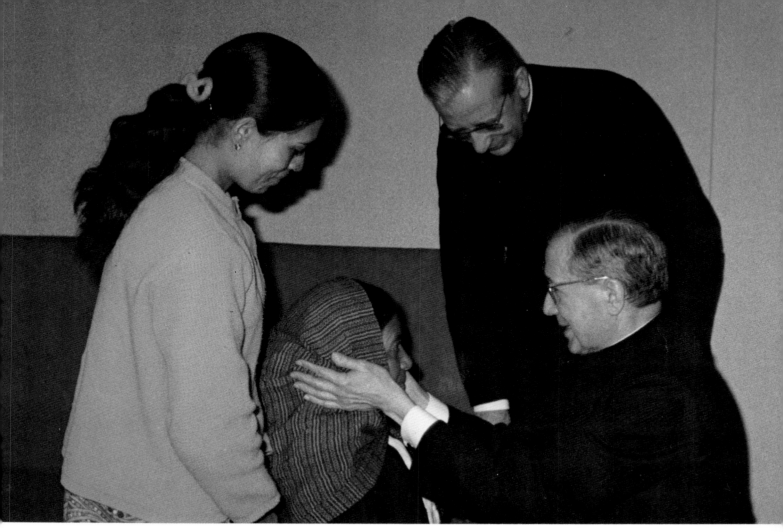

[52] GRATEFUL MOTHER MEETS THE FATHER

During his trip to Mexico in 1970, the founder met, among others, many of the parents of Mexican members. Above he is seen greeting an Indian woman, mother of four members of the Work. Also visible are her daughter Victoria and Father del Portillo. When Monsignor Escrivá approached to greet her, she fell on her knees out of gratitude and respect. "None of that, my daughter, none of that," was his immediate response as he too knelt on the floor, adding, "We are all equal, my daughter, all of us are God's children...."

many apostolic instruments come into being. He was also concerned that in each new country Opus Dei become "a pastoral phenomenon native to that country," while still retaining its essential identity. Besides, he was bent on expanding apostolic ventures in favor of the poor.

These projects are what Opus Dei calls corporate works. As we have seen, the value of an academy or student residence was not lost on the founder. Such institutions were means—not ends—that facilitated and multiplied apostolic friendships, while they also assured continuity and focus. With Monsignor Escrivá in the wings, a wide range of educational and beneficent undertakings were born: schools, universities [49], vocational training centers, medical dispensaries, housekeeping schools....These were to be professionally run, non-profit operations offering a service to the local community and thereby reflecting Opus Dei's spirit of human excellence and Christian dedication.

There too members and their friends (and their friends) could attend spiritual conferences and classes, go for confession and spiritual guidance, participate in days of recollection and retreats. Thus a student might go from a class in computers to another in Christian living—and in the latter course be told,

There were also get-togethers with students during Monsignor Escrivá's trip to Mexico in 1970. One day a large group of high school and college students joined him on an outdoor patio at the Pan-American University Residence in Mexico City. Before they met, however, the heavens opened and an awning was strung over the patio. Since no canvas is perfect, they gave the founder, along with a microphone, an umbrella, as we see here.

among other things, how important it was for him to develop his talents fully.

From Rome Monsignor Escrivá closely followed these grassroots efforts. When other commitments allowed, the founder would take to the road on brief, intense trips, always combined with private pilgrimages to shrines dedicated to Mary [44, 47]. "We have filled the highways of Europe with Hail Marys and songs," he used to comment. These trips would allow the founder to see and encourage members who were breaking ground, often hard ground. He would also find new grist for his reflection and prayer. At other times he would meet in Rome with representatives from the various nations where Opus Dei was at work to study questions related to the apostolate. From these fact-finding visits and sessions would come helpful directives.

In June, 1957, Carmen, the founder's sister, died in Rome at age 57 [45]. Two months earlier physicians had told her she had cancer of the liver. She never married; she was always too busy helping her brother,

principally with the women's branch. From after the Spanish war until well into the fifties she had taken charge of organizing the domestic services at a succession of new centers. "It was very good for us," acknowledged Monsignor Escrivá, "that my mother and my sister Carmen willingly took over the housekeeping chores of our first centers. Especially Carmen, who got involved in everything. If not, we would not have had a true home: it would have turned out to be some kind of barracks."

After Spain and Italy, Opus Dei's founder spent the most time in England, where he passed part of each summer from 1958 to 1962 [46]. He went to give a hand where the going was a bit slow. He saw lots of people; he opened doors; he visited many Marian shrines; he fanned projects and start-ups in new cities. That first summer, however, while visiting the City of London (the British equivalent of Wall Street), he was temporarily overcome by a feeling of impotence in the face of such diversity, wealth and power. Taking refuge in prayer, he heard deep in his soul, "You can't; I can!"

This was not the first time God had spoken to him —nor the last. The founder rarely talked about these special favors. For him the greatest miracle was to do ordinary things extraordinarily well; for the rest, "there are more than enough miracles recorded in the Gospel." Nevertheless, he did admit on one occasion, "When they were necessary, there have been extraordinary interventions of God, which scared me. If I said the contrary, I would lie. When they happened, I would immediately feel his 'It is I'."

Meanwhile Opus Dei was growing not only "within." Sometime in the forties membership reached one thousand; within the next decade it totaled ten thousand. During Vatican Council II it had increased to 25,000. It more than doubled during the next decade, with members of more than 80 nationalities. Yet Monsignor Escrivá, who put little stock in numbers and statistics, insisted that Opus Dei was very young

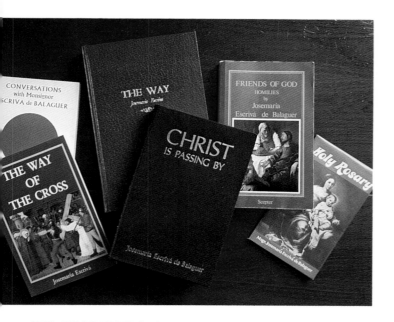

[54] 'ESCRIVÁ' MEANS SCRIBE

Shown are the founder's works available in English (published by Scepter Press). *Holy Rosary*, written in one sitting in 1934, offers commentary on the 15 mysteries. *The Way*, a primer for meditation, was first published in 1939; an earlier version was issued in 1934 as *Spiritual Considerations. Conversations with Monsignor Escrivá*, a compilation of press interviews, appeared in 1968. A series of homilies on major liturgical feasts and seasons, *Christ Is Passing By* was first issued in 1973. Published posthumously in 1977, *Friends of God* is another collection of homilies, dealing largely with virtues. Another posthumous work, *The Way of the Cross*, features commentaries and meditations on the 14 stations of the cross. Today, their combined circulation exceeds five million copies. Numerous homilies, letters and other writings remain to be published.

[55] FIRST FRUITS FROM AFRICA

Monsignor Escrivá never made it to Africa himself, but he sent members to Kenya as early as 1958 and Nigeria in 1965. Here we see some of the results: a few African members gathered in Rome, along with members and friends from around the world. These Holy Week visits to Rome, starting in the late '60's, soon became a tradition among young people of the Work.

In Kenya Opus Dei was in the forefront of breaking the color barrier: Strathmore College, for men, and Kianda College, for women, were among the first interracial educational ventures in all of East Africa, thanks in large part to the deployment of English-speaking members from the United States, Ireland and Great Britain.

[56] ANOTHER 'CATECHETICAL' JOURNEY

Back in the '30s the founder had written, "Agreed: you do better work with that friendly chat or that heart-to-heart conversation than with making speeches...in public before thousands of people. Nevertheless, when speeches have to be made, make them." During what he called a "catechetical" trip to Portugal and Spain in 1972, Monsignor Escrivá delivered neither speeches nor sermons, but he did speak to many: over 150,000 in two months, in a family-style format that grew out of earlier trips.

Here he speaks to an estimated 6,000 in a gymnasium in Barcelona.

[57] WITH 'THE TREASURE OF THE CHURCH'

Opus Dei's founder blesses cloistered Carmelites through the grill of their convent in Puzol, near Valencia, Spain, during his 1972 trip. At their initiative, he visited several communities of Carmelites and other contemplative nuns. Several years earlier he told a journalist: "Opus Dei has always enjoyed the admiration and sympathetic good will of religious of many orders and congregations, especially of enclosed monks and nuns, who pray for us, write to us often, and make our work known in a thousand ways, for they can appreciate the meaning of our life as contemplatives in the midst of the cares of everyday life."

After his death a Spanish Carmelite superior wrote with regard to his spiritual writings: "[They] lead us to God, they unite us to Jesus Christ, they make us love our Creator more and pray more for all the creatures on the earth. In letting ourselves be led by the hand of this holy founder, in whom Christ lived in an intense way, many of us have experienced a kind of renewed fervor to live our spirit."

[58] APOSTOLATE WITH PRIESTS

In his various trips Monsignor Escrivá eagerly met with fellow diocesan priests, even though he likened it to "selling honey to a beekeeper." Through the Priestly Society of the Holy Cross he had always sought to offer them fraternal friendship, spiritual encouragement and a spirituality that respected their secular (diocesan) status.

Here we see him in Madrid in 1972. He spoke to them, among other spiritual themes, of keeping their life of piety alive, of "wasting time" on God and his Mother. Always one to offer graphic examples, he showed his confreres how, in the consecration at Mass, he liked to make the genuflexion called for by the rubrics in a dignified way.

[59] 1974-75: IN LATIN AMERICA

Another catechetical trip in 1974 led Monsignor Escrivá to spend three summer months in South America: Brazil, Argentina, Chile, Peru, Ecuador and Venezuela. In February, 1975, he was in Venezuela and Guatemala. Get-together after get-together, more visits to Marian shrines.... At times he was so hoarse he could barely speak. But speak he did, to hundreds of thousands: about prayer, the sacraments (especially confession), about loving the Pope, traditional devotions.... Here, while Father del Portillo looks on, we see him kissing medals of the Virgin Mary attached to each decade of his rosary.

and small. He used to say that "a year in the life of an institution destined to last till the end of time was equivalent to a minute in the life of a newborn baby."

From his Roman home he felt impelled to identify himself more and more with the successor of St. Peter —"whoever he is"—and the needs of the universal Church [48]. Part of his eagerness to see men and women members spend several years at his side arose from his desire that they receive an indelible Roman and therefore catholic imprint. In 1957 Pius XII entrusted to some Opus Dei priests a mission territory that no other Catholic institution wanted. As a result priests of Opus Dei took charge of the Prelature of Yauyos, high in the Peruvian Andes, a region destitute in resources and, until then, spiritually neglected.

In many ways Monsignor Escrivá contributed to the Second Vatican Council. At the Vatican's request, he made fully available Opus Dei's secretary general, Father Alvaro del Portillo, before and during the Council. Many high ecclesiastics, thanks to this exposure, or to the presence of Opus Dei members in their dioceses, came to recognize in Opus Dei's founder a "precursor" of the essential teachings of Vatican II. Many of the Council's teachings or emphases were already established practice in Opus Dei. It is no wonder then that many participants in the Council sought out Monsignor Escrivá to hear his views.

Once one of the bishops pointed out to him that the Council was coming to see that the task of lay people was to bring a Christian leaven to secular structures in order to transform them. While assenting to the general formulation, Monsignor Escrivá emphatically laid down a condition: "If they have a contemplative soul, your excellency. Otherwise they won't transform anything; rather they'll be trans-

[60] A LAST 'FOLLY'

The year 1984 marked the ninth centenary of the shrine of Our Lady of Torreciudad. In 1084, according to ancient records, the carved, Romanesque statue was again enthroned in what was part of a Moorish fortress to celebrate one of the early victories over the Muslims in the Reconquest that was to end in 1492. Here in 1904 the founder, then two, was brought in pilgrimage by his parents to thank the Virgin for having spared their baby son. At that time, however, the trio from nearby Barbastro would have seen on this spot only a barren, rocky hilltop as they made their way to the old shrine.

The hilltop was leveled off in the late 1960s to make way for a new home for that poplar-hewn image of the seated Madonna who from her lap offers her Son. Some six years later, thanks to the founder's faith and gratitude, plus the generosity of thousands the world over, the shrine opened its gates. By 1986 it had attracted over 3 million pilgrims. "The miracles I would like to see (at Torreciudad) are conversions and peace brought to many souls," the founder specified. In three crypt chapels under the main church are found—and used—40 confessionals.

The photograph was taken from one of the two walkways leading to the entrance gates. Just within the gates begins a huge esplanade. The angled arcades that lead to the church on either side provide walkways on top and images of the 15 mysteries of the rosary underneath. Not shown is a path on the left leading to the old shrine. On the way pilgrims pass tiled representations of the seven joys and sorrows of St. Joseph. The church itself is of modern, simple design, made entirely of bare brick and roof tiles; its silhouette resembles the Pyrenean foothills it graces. Towering above is a 13-bell carillon. Flanking the church on the left and behind are two retreat houses and two centers: one for training area women in domestic sciences and another for local historical research.

Neither within the gates nor for a mile or two outside them is there anything commercial. The founder explained why: "People will go there to pray, to honor the blessed Virgin and seek the paths of God, not to buy knick-knacks. I don't like seeing the house of God turned into a bazaar."

If the founder considered Torreciudad to be one of his last "follies," as he put it, he always dreamed that Opus Dei would raise up other such shrines throughout the world, including one in the United States.

formed. Instead of making the world Christian, they'll just become mundane." Later another high churchman mentioned that lay people are charged with the mission of ordering secular institutions according to the divine will. "Yes, that's right," interposed the founder, "but first they have to be well ordered within: men and women of a profound interior life, souls of prayer and sacrifice. If not, instead of ordering family and social realities, they'll bring to them their own personal disorder."

The founder was pleased to see the Council solemnly confirm fundamental aspects of the Work's spirituality [50], such as the universal call to holiness and the response to it amid everyday occupations, professional work as a means to sanctity and apostolate, the legitimate freedom of lay people in temporal questions, the holy Mass as the "center and root" of Christian life.

But not all was light in the aftermath of the Council. Even Pope Paul VI was led to speak of "the decomposition of the Church." Monsignor Escrivá was anything but indifferent to the post-conciliar problems. While taking whatever measures were necessary within Opus Dei to assure its fidelity to the Council's authentic teachings, he felt a painful solicitude for the whole Church. "I suffer an incredible amount," he wrote in 1970. "We are living in a moment of madness. Millions upon millions of souls are confused. There is a great danger that in practice the sacraments will be drained of their content: all of them, including baptism. And the commandments of God's law are losing their meaning in men's consciences."

In response Monsignor Escrivá invited members and friends alike to join him in a renewed commitment to prayer and reparation. In fact, the erosion and attrition afflicting the Church were largely to motivate the founder's activities for the rest of his days.

Monsignor Escrivá turned ever more to the blessed Virgin. He felt a growing urge to visit her shrines in a succession of private penitential pilgrimages [47]. Thus we find him in the late '60s laying his concerns at the feet of his Mother at various shrines in Italy, Switzerland, France, Spain....In 1970, after visiting, among others, the shrine at Fatima, he continued westward to Mexico City where he made a novena— praying several hours a day for nine days—before the Virgin of Guadalupe [64].

He prolonged that first trip to the Western hemisphere for another month in what he called a catechetical journey [51]. Several times a day he would receive large groups of people in a family-like gathering where members and friends would share with him what was on their minds [52, 53]. He, in turn, would answer them to the point, explaining, cajoling, giving doctrine, opening vistas for generosity, speaking clearly about dangers and remedies, always acting the priest, with never a lament or criticism. In this fashion he saw thousands, including many from beyond Mexico's borders. This format was to characterize his remaining trips.

His pastoral concern also led him to publish more [54].

In 1972 he resumed direct pastoral work, dedicating two months to another catechetical trip to Portugal and Spain [56], where he spoke on hundreds of occasions to over 150,000 men and women, boys and girls, professionals and workers, laity and clergy [58]. His message was demanding—prayer and the sacraments, work and the duties of one's state in life—but wrapped in such affection, understanding, good humor and encouragement that many were moved to apply themselves to their Christian vocation anew or for the first time.

Convinced that they "are the treasure of the Church," Monsignor Escrivá also visited cloistered nuns, at their invitation, in various Iberian cities [57]. To one such group he said, "Not long ago I wrote to a

[61] ORDINATIONS AT THE SHRINE

Since the Torreciudad shrine was opened in 1975, it has played host to many of the yearly ordinations of Opus Dei priests from throughout the world. Over 300 of the Work's priests have been ordained here beneath the gaze of Our Lady of Torreciudad, enshrined in the niche found just beneath the crucifix in the altarpiece. The ordination ceremony of August, 1978, is pictured here.

The church has a single nave in which both walls and vault conspire to rivet one's attention on the altarpiece and in particular the central tabernacle window from which the blessed sacrament presides over the whole shrine. Beneath the tabernacle and above the 11th century Madonna is a crucifixion scene. The uppermost central panel shows Mary being crowned by the blessed Trinity. From the top, the left panels depict her betrothal to Joseph, the annunciation and her visit to Elizabeth; those on the right show the nativity with shepherds, the flight into Egypt and the holy family in Joseph's workshop.

The three-quarter relief, life-sized figures are delicately polychromed. They are carved from alabaster, a material quarried in that part of Spain. While a modern masterpiece, the work is inspired by traditional altarpieces common in the former kingdom, now province, of Aragon.

[62] THE EAGER, DELIGHTED FOUNDER

Monsignor Escrivá is shown contemplating the altarpiece of the shrine of Our Lady of Torreciudad in May, 1975, alongside an equally delighted Father del Portillo. It was the first time he had seen the nearly completed work. He exclaimed at the time, "What sighs this will draw from old women...and from young people! What sighs! Only the crazy folks of Opus Dei do this, and we're very happy to be crazy...."

diocesan bishop, giving him as it were my condolences over the closing of a convent of Capuchin nuns who had been in that diocese for centuries. I told him, 'What a pity; you're going to be left without strength.' How is he, alone, going to bear up under the weight of those souls, those sheep, if he cannot count on the strength of souls dedicated to the Lord in the cloister? I have said that you nuns are a thousand times blessed, and it makes me happy to repeat it a thousand times over."

Starting in the late '60s, groups of young people in contact with Opus Dei—first from Germany, then from throughout Europe, finally from around the globe—launched the custom of spending Holy Week in Rome [55], with a little encouragement and a lot of attention from Monsignor Escrivá. They too should make their pilgrimage *videre Petrum*: to see the Pope. At one such gathering in 1973, numbering several thousand, the founder again displayed his knack for drawing young people. "If you are here," he told them, "it's because you're rebels, the good kind. Unfortunately, in the world, the biggest push is downwards. People talk without pause about sexual matters, violence, making money at any cost, turning their backs on others. But they don't speak about God. You, however, who realize that the world is trying to get you to live like animals, have answered: No, we don't want to be animals. You have rebelled against all that, and you wish to love God a lot, God who is your Father. You are the greatest rebels I know. Foster that rebellion which pleases God our Lord so much."

During 1974 Monsignor Escrivá spent over three months in South America [59]: Brazil, Argentina, Chile, Peru, Ecuador and Venezuela. On the last leg of the trip, starting in Peru, he took sick, in part because of the high altitude. However, he still spoke to thousands in Peru, Ecuador and Venezuela. The interrupted trip was resumed in February, 1975, with visits to Venezuela and Guatemala, though sickness and exhaustion returned to dog him.

Monsignor Escrivá never proposed himself as a model—except in one thing: "the love I have for the Virgin." If in that area he was determined "not to be outdone," he outdid himself in converting a near-abandoned shrine of Mary's, high in the foothills of the Pyrenees and dating back some thousand years [4], into a powerful magnet of popular devotion. In late spring, 1975, he visited the nearly completed shrine of Torreciudad [60] to see the new church and its striking altarpiece, carved out of alabaster, which feature the age-darkened Madonna and Child [61, 62]. He also inaugurated the shrine's 40 confessionals, whence would come "spiritual miracles."

Torreciudad also reflects the founder's aversion to anything resembling stinginess when it comes to divine worship. "People in love," he said repeatedly, "don't give each other pieces of iron or bags of cement. They give precious things: the best they have. When the world's lovers change their way of acting, so will we."

By this "folly," Opus Dei's founder was trying to repay a favor from the blessed Virgin that reached him so early in life that he was not aware of it until at age 11 his mother told him. When Josemaría was barely two, he fell ill (with what, we don't know). It was bad enough, in any case, that two physicians concurred that the illness was likely to prove fatal in short order. In one of his subsequent visits the family doctor said, "He won't last the night." When his mother heard this, she put the matter in the Virgin's hands. She promised that if her son was cured, she would take him on pilgrimage to the out-of-the-way shrine of Torreciudad. When the family doctor returned first thing in the morning to offer his condolences, he found a completely restored Josemaría jumping up and down.

THE CLOSE

[63] MORE THAN A SUMMERTIME FAREWELL

In the last photograph taken of Monsignor Escrivá, he is seen greeting members at the Roman College of Holy Mary in suburban Castelgandolfo. He told the women present: "…I will tell you as I do whenever I come here that you, by the simple fact of being Christians, have priestly souls. With your priestly soul and with God's grace, you can and should help the priestly ministry that we priests carry out. Together we shall work effectively.

"In everything you do, find a reason to talk to God and to his Blessed Mother, who is our mother, and to St. Joseph, our father and lord, and to our guardian angels, so as to help this holy Church, our mother, who is in such great need, and who is having such a difficult time in the world these days. We should love the Church and the Pope very much. Ask our Lord that our service on behalf of the Church and the Pope may be effective…."

[64] 'THE WAY I'D LIKE TO DIE'

From the earliest days Monsignor Escrivá had the custom, shared with members of Opus Dei, of always glancing at an image of the blessed Virgin on entering or leaving a room. On entering his workroom just before he died, he undoubtedly looked at an image of the Virgin of Guadalupe hanging opposite the door.

Shown is a photograph of the original image of Our Lady of Guadalupe, before which the founder made a novena in 1970 in Mexico City. Tradition explains its origin: one day in the early 16th century the Virgin appeared to the Indian Juan Diego to entrust him with the mission of persuading the bishop to raise up a shrine. After his first attempts, the bishop asked the Indian to request a sign that would prove the authenticity of the apparition. So the blessed Virgin one December day deposited some unseasonal roses in the Indian's cloak to take to the bishop as the requested proof. When Juan Diego opened his cloak in the prelate's presence, there appeared this image miraculously imprinted on his garment, an object of great devotion throughout Mexico since that time.

During his 1970 visit to Mexico, the founder gathered with a large group of diocesan priests at a conference center near Guadalajara. The get-together was lively and long, the weather warm, leaving Monsignor Escrivá worn out. Father del Portillo convinced him to rest a while. From a bed the founder could see a painting of the Virgin placing roses in Juan Diego's cloak. Gazing at it, the founder was heard to say: "That's the way I'd like to die: looking at the Virgin who's giving me a rose."

For a number of years the founder had prayed for a death that would allow him to work to the very end, "without creating a bother." Aside from the sick spells in Latin America, Monsignor Escrivá was in good health and as active as ever.

He was seeing to the completion not only of Torreciudad, but of another "folly" of his: a village-like complex of buildings to house the Opus Dei men attending the Roman College of the Holy Cross. They had outgrown their temporary facilities at the organization's headquarters.

In the spring of 1975, now in his 74th year, Monsignor Escrivá marked the golden anniversary of his ordination. There was no fanfare. In fact, since the day fell on Good Friday, when Mass is not celebrated, he was not able to renew the sacrifice of the altar. Whether or not he sensed that the end might be near, on various occasions during the first half of 1975 he would off-handedly mutter that he was "only getting in the way."

Whenever possible in the summer, Father del Portillo would try to get the founder away from the op-

[65] WHERE HIS HEART GAVE OUT
Shown is the room where at midday on June 26, 1975, Monsignor Escrivá collapsed on the floor, under the crucifix, and died.

pressive heat in Rome to rest while working in a more congenial locale. As June came to a close, Monsignor Escrivá made plans to leave Rome for a spell. As usual, that called for a farewell visit to women and men members studying in Rome. He set aside the morning of June 26 to be with his spiritual daughters; in the afternoon he could visit the men.

That morning, midway through a get-together with women members in suburban Castelgandolfo [63], he felt weak and cut the session short. After resting a bit the founder felt well enough to ride back to Opus Dei's Roman headquarters, accompanied by two priests who were his inseparable aides: Alvaro del Portillo and Javier Echevarría.

In a long letter to Opus Dei members, Father del Portillo described the moment: "On entering from Bruno Buozzi [the street name] a few minutes before 12 noon, our Father greeted the Lord in the Father's Chapel with a slow, devout genuflection, accompanied by an act of love, as he usually did. Then we went up

to the room where he habitually worked—you all know that it is my office..." On entering the office he probably looked at an image of the Lady of Guadalupe [64].

"...Just after he crossed the threshold he called out, 'Javi!' [Father Javier Echevarría had stayed behind to close the elevator door.] The Father repeated louder still, 'Javi!' Then in a weaker voice, 'I don't feel well.' The Father immediately fell to the floor. By that time [Father] Joe Soria [a physician by training] and I were also in the room. We used all possible means, spiritual and medical. I gave him absolution and the anointing of the sick while he was still breathing. It was an hour and a half of struggle, of hopes: oxygen, injections, cardiac massages....We couldn't believe that the time had come for such a great sorrow.

"...We resisted the conviction that he had died [65]. For us certainly it came across as a sudden death. For the Father, without a doubt, it was something that had been taking shape—I dare to say—more in his soul

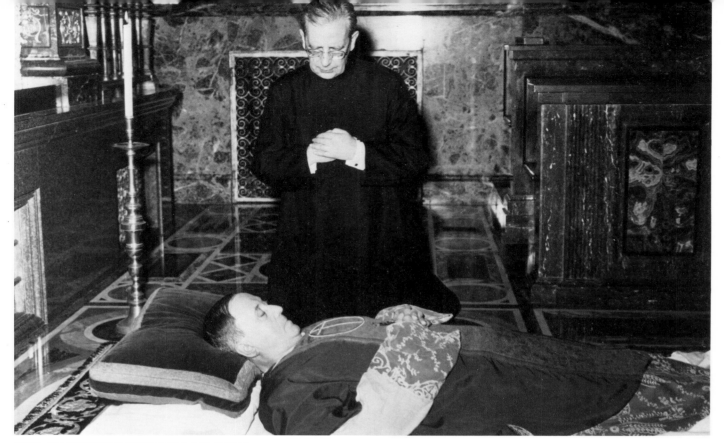

[66] AN 'ADIOS' (LITERALLY: 'TO GOD')

The founder was waked in the chapel of Our Lady of Peace in Opus Dei's headquarters. Father del Portillo is seen here in prayer at the side of the man by whom he had stood for 40 years. Members continued working; things went on as before. If anything, unity within the Work was reinforced.

On September 15, 1975, nearly three months afterwards, Father del Portillo (soon to be named Monsignor) was unanimously elected on the first ballot to succeed the late founder by representatives gathered in Rome from each of the 33 countries where Opus Dei was established at the time.

than in his body, because every day more frequently he offered up his life for the Church."

The founder was waked in the chapel of Our Lady of Peace in Opus Dei's headquarters [66]. A festive alb and chasuble were placed over his cassock. As soon as possible, Father del Portillo said the first of 51 continuous Masses for the repose of his soul during the hours before his burial.

Many came to mourn and pray during those serenely sad 26 hours: high churchmen, lowly workers, members of the Work, the founder's brother Santiago.... Commented a Roman Cardinal who knew Monsignor Escrivá well: "How much is he going to do for the Church from heaven!" On all six continents the 62,000 Opus Dei members prayerfully sought to decipher the application of *Omnia in bonum* ["all things work out for the best"], one of his favorite sayings, to the stark fact of his death.

In the afternoon of the following day, the body was placed in a mahogany coffin, which was sealed after the solemn funeral Mass celebrated by Father del Portillo. The coffin was then carried to the crypt below, where it was lowered into a tomb in the floor and sealed with a marble cover.

Raised letters on the slab give the dates of his birth and death and a two-word biography: "The Father."

GATHERING ECHOES

[67] MORE VISITORS THAN EVER

Today Monsignor Escrivá's tomb—if it would be inappropriate to call it a happy place—at the very least is a busy one. Every day hundreds of people, from Rome or out of town, come to pray for him, for themselves, for their loved ones. All kinds of people touch the marble cover, even kiss it as we see here, or place flowers, rosaries and other religious articles upon it while they pray. Meanwhile, in an adjoining building several stories up, someone is opening a stack of mail received earlier that day. From Poland alone, where Opus Dei cannot yet be established, come 20 to 40 letters a day. The letters are from grateful people who claim that through the founder's intercession they have received spiritual or material favors; some even speak of miracles. That's for the Church to decide in its ongoing study to determine whether the Spanish priest will be raised to the altars. But some of the letter writers will apparently need little convincing. A random sample:

"Several months ago I had a favor granted through the intercession of Monsignor Escrivá…I received a phone call from my grandmother informing me that she and my grandfather (both in their mid-80s and never married by the Church) were getting married in the Church that evening." "…My uncle became gravely ill and was taken to the hospital. I hadn't seen him in many years, but I knew that in religious matters he was apathetic, specifically with regard to confession. I began to commend the matter to Monsignor Escrivá, asking him not to let him die without confession and the last sacraments…The day we brought him a priest, he agreed to go to confession…." "Last month my uncle was kidnapped. They told us that they were going to kill him if he did not pay a certain amount of money. We were very worried. Then I remembered having read various favors received through the intercession of Monsignor Josemaría. We started a novena. Before finishing it, my uncle was freed…."